PAPAL ECONOMICS

ALSO AVAILABLE IN THE
CULTURE OF ENTERPRISE SERIES

PAPAL ECONOMICS

The Catholic Church on
Democratic Capitalism

MACIEJ ZIĘBA, OP

WILMINGTON, DELAWARE

In memory of Father Richard John Neuhaus (1936–2009)

For his great friendship and
intellectual precision and courage

Copyright © 2013 by Maciej Zięba, OP
First paperback printing, 2014

This English-language edition of *Papal Economics* was made possible by the generous support of Mr. Thomas Posatko. The Culture of Enterprise series is supported by a grant from the John Templeton Foundation. The Intercollegiate Studies Institute gratefully acknowledges this support.

Cataloging-in-Publication data is on file with the Library of Congress.
ISBN: 9781610171342

ISI Books
Intercollegiate Studies Institute
3901 Centerville Road
Wilmington, DE 19807
www.isibooks.org

Manufactured in the United States of America

CONTENTS

FOREWORD

by Michael Novak

For a long time to come, this book may well be the definitive work on the economic teaching of the modern popes. Over the course of more than a century, the papacy has appropriated into its own intellectual traditions a profound understanding of democracy and—a greater surprise—an appreciative understanding of capitalism. This effort came to maturity in the person of Pope John Paul II, who distinguished true democracy from false, and praiseworthy capitalism from the kind to be rejected.

Over this time the Catholic Church has shown itself far more open to new ideas in adapting itself to democracy and capitalism than secular liberals have been open to new ways of adapting to religious realities.

For one thing, during the past thirty years the "secularization thesis" has had to be abandoned—that is, the thesis whereby history is assumed to be moving in a secular direction, such that religion will soon disappear from the public stage. The opposite appears to be happening—religion is growing in size and influence—and with accelerating speed.

The numbers of the Catholic people around the world, for instance, have been growing at rapid rates. The raw number of Catholics now living on this planet is at an all-time high. There are more Methodists—just Methodists—on this planet today than there were all Christians together at the time of the "Great Schism" between Constantinople and Rome (in AD 1054). The explosive dynamism of worldwide Islam during this generation has by now forced itself on everyone's attention. And the numbers of evangelical Christians in Latin America, Africa, and Asia continue to zoom upward. Even formerly repressive atheist regimes in China and the former Soviet Union have been experiencing hundreds of thousands of conversions to the Christian faith.

John Paul II has deservedly been called "John Paul the Great." He received the accolade in large measure because of his startling success in undermining the moral ground on which the Communist systems were precariously built. But he is recognized for many other achievements as well—his cheerful persistence in pulling his bent body up into airplanes despite his evident Parkinson's disease, as a way of comforting the sick and the suffering and the aged everywhere; his World Youth Days all around the globe, which drew millions of young people; and his extensive and penetrating papal writings. John Paul the Great became the clearest voice in defending the human rights of peoples all around the world. He promoted democracy as well, which he saw to be a flawed system but, just the same, the safest political barrier against systemic abuses of human rights.

For all his greatness, Pope John Paul II was also a warm, humble, down-to-earth, good-humored person. He loved to invite people of all sorts, but especially friends, for early Mass with him, or for lunch or dinner. He just plain liked people.

THE POPE AND THE PRIEST

It so happened that partway through his pontificate, Pope John Paul II met in person with the young Dominican priest Father Maciej Zięba (pronounced: Zhiemba)—a Polish intellectual who had been a promising physicist until he helped edit an underground paper for the Polish trade union, Solidarność, and then recovered his faith and entered into the Dominican way of life, as scholar, spiritual adviser, and preacher. Zięba is a tall, large-boned, cheerful man, as full of jokes and good humor as he is of serious purpose and deep faith in the love of God. Anyone who visits Father Zięba's offices in the Tertio Millennio Institute in Krakow, Poland, will note with some surprise and admiration the many tokens of paternal esteem the pope showered upon him—framed letters, photos, icons, and small paintings given him as mementos down the years. Anyone who saw the two of them together in private settings would have noted immediately that the pontiff treated "Maciej" like a favorite nephew, breaking into a smile immediately on catching sight of him and trading ripostes with him. Father

Zięba was treated in the Vatican as part of the Holy Father's circle of friends, a favorite among them, perhaps because Father Zięba had, as the pope did, a certain dramatic flair, spiritual depth, and zest for life.

In Father Zięba's private study there was once upon a time a large photo of Chicago mayor Richard J. Daley Sr., put there partly in jest by his fellow Dominicans, who by uncommon organization got Father Zięba elected twice as provincial superior for the entire Polish Province of Dominicans. Notwithstanding all these additional administrative burdens, Father Zięba was fiercely determined to finish his doctoral thesis in theology on a matter of public intellectual life and social, political, and economic importance in Poland at that time: Catholic social doctrine and its early hesitations and fears regarding both capitalism and democracy. Here Father Zięba was thinking along with John Paul.

It was easy for Zięba, an intellectual, a physicist by training, a man close to the young and to the growth and broad appeal of Solidarność during a crucial period for Lech Walesa, to grasp the connection between democratic institutions and the protection of human rights. It was easy for him, too—a matter of daily observation—to recognize the fallacies and impracticalities in socialist economics. As for capitalism? Well, not many in Poland during the fifty years of Communist denigration of capitalism, or even under the long history of resistance, were parties to "vulgar" commerce. What Poles learned to admire about capitalism came from background scenes in American films, showing the heavily laden meat coolers in the gleaming supermarkets, the casual, well-dressed people, the quiet automobiles gliding down every street. If capitalism was a morally ugly system—as all authorities seemed to say—it certainly seemed to work to the good of ordinary people.

Then, too, a huge proportion of Polish families had at least one relative, perhaps a distant relative, living somewhere in the United States, who would from time to time send photos and sometimes money. Not a few older Poles now back in Poland still collect U.S. social security checks from their younger years of working in America. To other Poles, they seemed very wealthy.

I will never forget the day when the young Father Zięba, in the United States for research, appeared nervously at my office door at the American Enterprise Institute (AEI). These were still the days of Communist control in Poland. As he told me later, he really felt frightened, partly for damage to his reputation in Poland. What if AEI turned out to be a CIA center? What if Michael Novak, who wrote about capitalism and democracy, turned out to be an agent of the Devil himself, aiming to sow confusion and materialistic destruction in the Church? Not only Communists but also anti-Western reactionaries in the Polish church openly expressed those views. Zięba did know that Solidarność, despite being a socialist labor union, had courageously published an underground translation of my book *The Spirit of Democratic Capitalism*. This did not entirely reassure him.

At the time, I had no real idea of Father Zięba's fears. I could certainly see that he was nervous. I remember now only that we had a very good talk and then agreed that he should come back over to AEI for some of the public discussions we had. He found it interesting that such a secular organization would want a theologian in the intellectual mix and that in public debate it was all right for me to be fairly explicit about my theological beliefs.

He attended one of our evening discussions on theology and economics among professors of theology and ethics from all the local seminaries and universities. There would be, we could all easily predict, a new papal encyclical on economic systems in 1991, to mark the hundredth anniversary of the first such encyclical, *Rerum Novarum*, in 1891. After all, under Pius XI there had been a fortieth-anniversary encyclical, and under Paul VI an eightieth-anniversary recollection. The question before this ongoing AEI seminar was, If the Vatican invited *you* to send in advice, what would you write? We heard from socialists, liberation theologians, liberal economists, and a few (there were only a few) theologians in favor of the free economy. We carried on this seminar about four times every year for a good many years. The seminar was great training for seeing the various sides of every issue—and the strong passions attached to them.

EXAMINING PAPAL THOUGHT ON CAPITALISM

As a grown man, Maciej had returned to his childhood faith. While working for Solidarność, he began to feel a call to become a priest. He had great admiration for the Dominican Order ("the order of preachers"), in part because of its emphasis on deep scholarship and on preaching, and in part because of its combination of the contemplative with the active priestly life. He proved to be gifted in his capacities as a spiritual director and confessor. He has an exceedingly quick and deep mind. He is an eloquent preacher, talking the language of common sense and common experience, but with a depth of insight into the knowledge and love of Christ that one does not often find. Before very long, he was made head of the Dominican publishing house, and some years later the editor of the Sunday supplement in the most widely distributed Catholic newspaper in Poland. He was often on radio broadcasts and with increasing frequency interviewed on television. In fact, he became the number one television commentator each time Pope John Paul II visited Poland. A very popular book was made of his longer commentaries about the pope. Father Zięba's articles soon began appearing in France, Germany, and the United States.

I am not certain how or where Father Zięba first met the pope, but I do know that it sufficed to bring a smile of affection to the pope's face if one merely mentioned Maciej's name. As the years went on, when Maciej was in Rome, he was often invited to the pope's table for lunch or dinner. The two had many other contacts as well. The young Dominican was invited two or three times to the annual summer seminars that the pope held at Castel Gandolfo for prominent intellectuals from around the world—once a meeting on physics and, on another occasion, to present a paper on the papal teaching on economics, particularly capitalism. (At least once the pope said to him afterward, "Did I write that?" Father Zięba told him, "Yes.") Not infrequently, letters from the pope would arrive in Krakow, or a small icon or photograph would appear.

From the very first, Father Zięba was invited to join the Summer Seminar on the Free Society that Rocco Buttiglione and I cooked up. Rocco was a professor of metaphysics at the Academy of Philosophy in Liechtenstein and also at the University of Social Sciences (LUISA) in Rome. He had gone to Poland as a young doctor of philosophy to study the phenomenology of ethics and aesthetics that had been developed over two decades by the Polish School, including Lublin University's Father Karol Wojtyla, later the archbishop of Krakow. Rocco learned Polish and became close to the young archbishop, who had already made something of a name for himself, even internationally, at the Second Vatican Council. Wojtyla intervened with Pope Paul VI, arguing with urgency on behalf of the bishops of Eastern Europe for the necessity of the Declaration of Religious Liberty, which was at that point stalled in the council. According to some authors, that intervention helped persuade the pope to order the draft declaration to the floor quickly before time ran out for final consideration and passage.

Curiously enough, Wojtyla was well placed enough on the council's drafting committee on the subject of the Church in the modern world to outargue the famous American proponent of religious liberty John Courtney Murray, SJ. Murray had wanted the document to be political and pragmatic so as to avoid interminable arguments over the philosophy of liberty. The declaration ought to be, Murray thought, a set of "articles of peace" between contending parties, which would protect the rights of all pragmatically. By contrast, Wojtyla joined with some of the theologians of the "nouvelle theologie" at the council, including Henri de Lubac, SJ, the brightest light of France and maybe of all Europe. Their view was that the declaration should be rooted in the long scriptural and traditional teaching about the radical freedom of the act of faith. In this act, each single person must make his or her own choice to accept or to reject the friendship that God offers to all. Neither mother nor father, nor brother nor sister, can make that choice of personal conscience. This approach, they thought, would ground the declaration in unimpeachable Catholic theology and thus ensure its longevity no matter what the pragmatic situation of one region or one time. On this point, the Europeans prevailed, even though most credit for the introduction of the theme of religious liberty into the council—and for carrying the early stages of the debate—was for many years given to the Americans.

When, in 1978, Cardinal Wojtyla was suddenly and dramatically elected pope, the first non-Italian pope in many centuries, he asked young Professor Buttiglione to relocate to Rome and give a hand on various matters of theological/social policy that had large philosophical components. Rocco could also help the pope find his early footing in respect to political life in Italy.

It had been Rocco's idea that some sort of new institution needed to be set up between Americans and Europeans, particularly the Italians and the Eastern Europeans. Both of us worried about the growing gap between European and American intellectual life and the relative isolation of the Church from the American experience. At first we explored the idea of a think tank or regularly meeting seminar in Italy, to which prominent scholars from both continents would be invited. After Pope John Paul II's astonishing encyclical *Centesimus Annus* in the spring of 1991, Josef Seifert, the founder and director of the International Academy of Philosophy, invited us to hold a month-long seminar in Liechtenstein. We decided to invite two-thirds of the participants from among Central and Eastern Europe young professionals who had never had a chance to study the classics of freedom (Tocqueville, *The Federalist Papers*, etc.), intermixed with about one-third from the United States and a handful from Western Europe. For two happy years we met in Liechtenstein.

Then through Rocco and Father Zięba, who had been invited from the first to join the small faculty, Pope John Paul II encouraged us to move the seminar to Poland, either to Lublin or to Krakow. (Derek Cross, who did much of the editing on the English edition of this book, first scouted out those two possible sites and with considerable wisdom recommended the location in Krakow—where, after two summers, he discovered his own vocation to the priesthood.) We have been meeting in the Dominican monastery in Krakow every summer since.

It was through Father Zięba, too, that George Weigel, another member of our faculty, expanded his already substantial list of Polish contacts, in preparation for the biography of Pope John Paul II that became a worldwide classic. We have always counted our little seminar as one providential means by which George's contacts with the Holy Father increased.

Through Father Zięba, the pope often wrote short (sometimes handwritten) notes to members of the seminar to encourage us in our work. I remember one year when he wrote that he admired the dedication of the young people to study the free society for a summer—at the same age, he said, he would have been hiking in the mountains or kayaking. He thanked us also for studying *Centesimus Annus* when not even many bishops were studying it. "Well, what can you do?" I seem to remember the pope's note concluding. (The little letter, framed, hangs on the wall of Father Zięba's office in Krakow.)

For the opening of the Holy Year in Rome in 2000, the alumni and former teachers of the seminar went to Rome, under George's leadership. The pope's staff saw to it that we were given ample tickets to the main events, plus the opportunity to meet privately with the pope himself. More than 130 alumni showed up. Already rather weakened by some wasting disease, the pope spent more than an hour with us, blessing each of us one by one or, in the case of couples, two by two. Our whole group had practiced a Polish Christmas carol for the occasion and sang it for him as a sign of gratitude—and the old man broke into a grin and sang along with us, directing the music with his hand.

Not every year, but often enough, we would receive, via Father Zięba, a letter of greetings and gratitude from the pope. Once when other faculty members had lunch with him in Rome, for which I was absent, he sent me greetings, saying, "Michael says he is Slovak, but he is really Polish." My friends got a kick out of that. I sent him a note saying that, although by his magisterium I may be Polish (which I took to be, from him, a high compliment), both genetically and by the village of my grandparents' origins I had to affirm again that I was Slovak. The next time I visited my grandfather's village, however, I read on a plaque in back of the Castle of Spišské Podhradie, for which the Novaks worked as serfs, that "these eleven counties of Slovakia had belonged to Poland from" 1475 until 1770, or some such dates. So I felt obliged to send the pope another card saying, "You were right again, and I was wrong. Darn that infallibility!"

But none of us competed, except possibly George, for the special care the Holy Father manifested toward Father Zięba. Through Father Zięba—since Dominican business often required him to go to Rome—one Christmas the pope even sent, by hand delivery, blessed *oblatky* (unleavened wafers) for his "American friends" so that we might each break the bread with our families over the holidays, according to the old Slavic Middle-European custom. The pope also began putting pressure on Father Zięba, even though the latter had been elected provincial superior of the Polish Province, to work speedily to finish his doctorate. That work is reflected in the book the reader now holds in his hands.

The text is sometimes dense and deep, in the manner of phenomenology in Poland, but it is also clear and commonsensical, the qualities Father Zięba most appreciated in American intellectual traditions. Only two dozen or so other Europeans, including Rocco Buttiglione, are as skilled in bridging the gap in understanding between Catholic Europe and Catholic America.

The main focus of this book is the history of Catholic social thought regarding the economic order. In that 120-year tradition, no pope has been so profound, and so in touch with the realities experienced by lay persons, as Pope John Paul II. No other book so well or so thoroughly discusses papal thought on capitalism. For helping Europeans and now, with this translation, Americans to see this history as a whole, and to appreciate the unique place John Paul the Great boldly seized within it, Father Zięba is to be warmly thanked.

MICHAEL NOVAK *is an author, a philosopher, and a theologian. He is visiting professor at Ave Maria University and for many years was the George Frederick Jewett Scholar in Religion, Philosophy, and Public Policy at the American Enterprise Institute.*

PAPAL ECONOMICS

Capitalism, Freedom, and Truth

On March 13, 2013, white smoke emerged from the chimney of the Sistine Chapel, signaling that the Catholic Church had elected a new pope. The latest successor of St. Peter was Cardinal Jorge Mario Bergoglio, archbishop of Buenos Aires, Argentina, who became known as Pope Francis. Initial reports focused on the firsts associated with his papacy: he was the first pope from the Americas, the first Jesuit pope, and the first pontiff to take the name Francis. Commentators quickly tried to gauge the direction the Church would take under Francis's leadership. Much of the speculation, particularly from the secular press, centered on how the new pope would address people of other religions, handle the Roman Curia, respond to abuse scandals within the Church, and treat issues such as same-sex marriage, abortion, and contraception.

Less discussed, but equally important, was the question

of how Pope Francis would influence Catholic social teaching. What is man's place in society, particularly in economic and political life? How should we regard the institutions of democratic capitalism that have become the model for so much of the world? These questions could not be ignored, especially given the damage wrought by the global economic crisis that began in 2007.

There is, in fact, a well-developed body of Catholic social teaching on the economic and political order. This teaching can be traced back to the social encyclical Pope Leo XIII issued in 1891, *Rerum Novarum*. In the more than 120 years since, Leo's successors have built on this encyclical with further teachings on capitalism and socialism, wealth and poverty, democracy and authoritarianism, and more. The importance of *Rerum Novarum* is reflected in the timing of several subsequent social encyclicals. For example, Pope Pius XI's *Quadragesimo Anno*—released in 1931, during the Great Depression—was published on the fortieth anniversary of Leo's landmark encyclical; *Mater et Magistra* (1961) commemorated the seventieth anniversary; Pope John Paul II's *Laborem Exercens* (1981), the ninetieth; and John Paul's *Centesimus Annus* (1991), the hundredth.

Other social encyclicals dealing with economics have appeared as well—including, in 2009, Pope Benedict XVI's *Caritas in Veritate*—but ultimately it is *Centesimus Annus* that stands out. John Paul's encyclical is at once in sync with a grand tradition of Catholic social thought and a work of real innovation, which is why it is the primary focus of this book.

To begin, *Centesimus Annus* provides the most comprehensive answer to a deceptively challenging question:

What is the Church's position on democratic capitalism? For decades commentators of all stripes have tried to enlist Catholic social teaching in their cause, variously arguing that it is left-wing or right-wing, pro-socialist or pro-capitalist, or even pro–"third way." Such interpretations illustrate what the Acton Institute's Samuel Gregg calls "the limits of applying secular political categories to something like the Catholic Church."[1]

This book aims to correct the misconceptions about the Church's teachings on economics. Although the teaching has evolved in certain important respects over more than a century, the social encyclicals display a continuity that many observers have missed. As early as *Rerum Novarum* in the nineteenth century, popes rejected socialism as wrong at its core—as "proposing a remedy far worse than the evil" it was designed to cure, in the words of *Quadragesimo Anno*. Moreover, it is clear, especially from *Centesimus Annus,* that a democratic state characterized by the rule of law and endowed with a market economy deserves praise and respect as a place in which human freedom can find expression.

Of course, this praise and respect cannot be unqualified. In taking a comprehensive approach, the encyclicals outline the dangers associated with democratic capitalism as well as the opportunities. In any case, the Church's teaching on economics and politics is not about endorsing particular social institutions or designing ones of a more "confessional" shape. It reminds us, more broadly, of the relationships between man, society, and the state and of the preeminence of culture over politics and economics.

Catholic social teaching thus makes an essential

contribution in moving beyond the narrow confines of secular discourse. The most serious dangers arise when the state and the market are elevated to absolutes in themselves—when man's spiritual dimensions are subordinated to his material ones. The market economy and the democratic order must operate in a larger culture that allows man to discover the transcendent dignity of each person and realize his humanity by giving himself to his fellow men and to God.

In short, the very survival of democratic capitalism depends on a culture rooted in transcendent truth. For, as Pope John Paul II suggests in *Centesimus Annus,* in a world without truth, freedom loses its meaning, the market loses its efficiency, and democracy yields to statism and even totalitarianism.

ONE

A Brief History of Democratic Capitalism in Catholic Social Teaching

Any attempt to analyze the continuity and evolution of the Catholic Church's social teachings on the subject of democratic capitalism is complicated by the fact that the popes have not often used the words *democracy* and *capitalism*. In trying to reconstruct the popes' views, one must draw on the numerous references in the encyclicals to the role of the state, socialism, liberalism, central planning, private ownership, and even the so-called third way—a Christian political-economic system that would challenge existing social solutions.

Rerum Novarum

Pope Leo XIII published the first social encyclical, *Rerum Novarum* (Of Revolution), on May 15, 1891. It was by no means clear at the time that the pope would support the existing political and economic system. Many liberal European states were trying to oust the Roman Catholic Church from the social sphere. The "worker question"— Leo's term for the increasingly combustible relationship between capitalist owners and wage laborers—threatened to explode the economic order. Finally, and probably most important, rapid social transformations and the erosion of the traditional code of values were bringing a veritable revolution.

Only in this context can the significance of *Rerum Novarum*'s rather cautious approval of the principles of capitalism be appraised. Oswald von Nell-Breuning, SJ, the distinguished expert on Catholic social teaching, discerned in this encyclical allusions to "an inquiry into the nature and causes of the wealth of nations," suggesting "some sympathy with Adam Smith."[1] Although the term *capitalism* does not appear in *Rerum Novarum*'s pages, Leo treats the then-extant form of capitalism as a system natural and right in principle, if in need of some correction in practice. The encyclical takes a different approach to the competing economic system. Socialism, the pope argues, is wrong at its core. Its psychological source is envy, while its aims—the complete equality of all humans, the abolition of private ownership, and "freedom from pain and trouble"—are utopian. Leo suggests that socialism will break society apart, bring harm to workers, and "rob the lawful possessor." Socialists "delude the people" and "bring forth evils worse than the present."[2]

Leo's view of the role of the state is complex. The pope—setting aside any concrete political system—treats the state, according to classical Thomist theory, as a *societas perfecta* responsible for realizing the common good.[3] This positive approach to the role of the state had, at the end of the nineteenth century, a particular meaning. On the one hand, it opposed the classical liberal ideal of the minimal state; on the other hand, it indirectly supported the freshly united Italian state, which was itself an example of the new, secular European regimes that had over the course of the nineteenth century replaced the church-allied monarchies of medieval Europe (a development often opposed directly by Church leadership, up to and including the pope).[4] We must therefore read the papal affirmations against the backdrop of a Church frequently failing to keep pace with rapid social changes and sometimes longing nostalgically for the ancien régime. Johannes Schasching, SJ, a leading European scholar of Catholic social teaching, notes: "In stressing the meaning of the state for the whole of industrialized society, the pope dispelled the feelings of mistrust many Catholics had towards the state; it stirred, however, in an entirely new way, a feeling of political responsibility."[5]

According to *Rerum Novarum,* the state should recognize the equality of all citizens, safeguard the interests of all, help realize both private and public prosperity, and advocate the improvement of the conditions of the working class through equitable distribution of property and through protection against all forms of exploitation. The state should also promote ownership and secure public peace. The means by which the state should accomplish these aims is seldom specified; this ambiguity leaves room for interpretation by those searching for support for political programs, left or right.

Natural law marks limits to state intervention, the encyclical says. Action that contravenes its rule, even if it claims to be for the good of the state, possesses not the power of law but only the power of force. (Here the pope cites St. Thomas Aquinas.) Government incursion into society should be carried out with no undue interference and within certain limits. State intrusion should not be based on raising taxes and other public obligations. The state should also respect the autonomy and property of the individual and the family, as both man and the family precede the state. The pope writes: "The contention, then, that the civil government should at its option intrude into and exercise intimate control over the family and the household is a great and pernicious error." State interventions cannot intend "to deprive citizens of their rights, but justly and properly to safeguard and strengthen them."[6]

Leo concludes, "The law must not undertake more, nor proceed further, than is required for the remedy of the evil or the removal of the mischief."[7] Thus, although the pope does not use the word *subsidiarity* in the encyclical, he seems to describe a state functioning according to the subsidiarity principle.[8] Pius XI would introduce that principle in its most common formulation in 1931, warning higher-level institutions such as the state against harmful interference in the life of more local communities such as the family. George Weigel, biographer of Pope John Paul II, defines subsidiarity as meaning "the community must not deprive individuals, nor larger communities deprive smaller communities, of the opportunity to do what they can for themselves."[9]

Pope Leo XIII views both the state and society from

an Aristotelian-Thomist perspective. This perspective is teleological and postulates a harmonious social life: "The purpose and perfection of an association is to aim at and to attain that for which it is formed, and its efforts should be put in motion and inspired by the end and object which originally gave it being." From this abstract pronounce- ment the pope moves to the level of social practice, discuss- ing the freedom to form associations and recognizing the positive role of various groups and associations mediating between the individual and the state. First among these is the family: "The family, the 'society' of a man's house—a society very small, one must admit, but none the less a true society, and one older than any State . . . consequently . . . has rights and duties peculiar to itself which are quite inde- pendent of the state."[10]

Leo places great emphasis on the formation of all kinds of associations: of laborers and employers (joint as well as individual organizations); educational, religious, and charitable organizations; and societies of citizens in gen- eral. "The State should watch over these societies of citi- zens banded together in accordance with their rights," the pope writes, adding, however—in another gesture toward subsidiarity—that it "should not thrust itself into their peculiar concerns and their organization." He writes, as well, about the right of citizens to choose their statutes, internal regulations, and self-managed organizational bases—something that deserves particular attention given the eminently holistic and teleological character of the pope's approach to social life: "We do not judge it possible to enter into minute particulars touching the subject of organization."[11] The entire range of circumstances, as well as the demands of the time and place, must be taken into consideration.

The pope's ideal vision of the harmonious cooperation of social groups and classes neither opposes private initiative nor weakens his awareness of real social problems. This ideal, modeled on the artisans' guilds of the Middle Ages, was very popular in the nineteenth-century Church, especially among Catholic social activists.[12] Leo notes the beauty of the concept but recognizes that at the close of the nineteenth century a medieval system could not be replicated exactly. Hence his comment, tinged with nostalgia, that "nothing more perfect had been known before, or will come to be known in the ages that have yet to be." Instead, he calls for an evolution of the old model: "Such unions should be suited to the requirements of this our age—an age of wider education, of different habits, and of far more numerous requirements in daily life."[13]

The pope then delicately—almost imperceptibly, if one does not take the statement in context—underlines his pluralistic vision: "It is gratifying to know that there are actually in existence not a few associations of this nature, consisting either of workmen alone, or of workmen and employers together, but it were greatly to be desired that they should become more numerous and more efficient."[14] This is a highly significant declaration. Studies on the genesis of *Rerum Novarum* reveal that just prior to publication of the encyclical, Leo personally added the phrase "either of workmen alone."[15]

It was a daring move to support the idea of the association of workers as stemming from natural law, as well as to underline the positive role of labor unions. The dominant

opinion in the ecclesiastical world held that the professional guilds were superior, and the era witnessed frequent,
even radical conflicts between employers and workers.
Moreover, the currents of the age—from the most moderate English trade unionism to anarchism, passing through
Lassallism in Germany, French and German social democracy, and revolutionary Marxism—ran in clear opposition
to the Catholic Church. Not only did these movements
proclaim anticlerical slogans, but also their fundamental
ideas challenged the foundations of faith and Christian
morality.

In the pages of *Rerum Novarum*, Leo argues that private property, like the right to form associations, stems
from natural law. The pope underscores the essential role
of private property by noting that it respects human reason
and the freedom of human nature, guarantees individual
autonomy, provides the foundation of public prosperity,
diminishes social divisions, releases industriousness, and
strengthens social stability. Although the pope distinguishes between "rightful ownership" and "rightful use" of
resources and their universal destination,[16] he emphasizes
the importance of private ownership by strongly criticizing communal property. Such an arrangement, the pope
argues, weakens initiative by eliminating the connection
between effort and reward. Thus it is unfair and harmful
for the worker, and damages free society.

In giving private property so much significance, Leo
breaks with the Thomist tradition, according to advocates
of both classical liberalism and socialism (arguing on
completely different grounds). This matter, in fact, became
a weighty controversy. But as the eminent social thinker

Cardinal Joseph Höffner has demonstrated, Leo's views are rooted in the teachings of St. Thomas, and any misunderstandings are terminological, not material.[17]

The pope's declared neutrality toward the political system of the state constitutes, in and of itself, a novelty in papal teaching. Some interpreters have read the encyclical as a subtle endorsement of democracy. "The social project formulated in *Rerum Novarum* seemed to some to be indivisible from a democratic-type political system," writes Patrick de Laubier, "while in the opinion of others it was only about necessary, partial social endeavors which it would be quite possible to reconcile with a traditional system."[18] These and other problems of social Catholicism led Leo to issue another encyclical ten years later on Christian democracy (in contrast to "social democracy"), *Graves de Communi Re*. Even then, however, the pope treated the subject of political democracy rather marginally. There he wrote, "It would be a crime to distort this name of Christian Democracy to politics." By the term *Christian democracy* he primarily meant charitable action conducted among the proletariat.

Although Leo did not deal with political systems in depth, he introduced the word *democracy* as a natural part of the language of the Church. This signaled a decisive shift from his predecessors: the acceptance of other forms of government besides the monarchic.

Rerum Novarum has been dubbed "the flagship of Catholic social teachings."[19] The label is deserved. In stormy and difficult times for the Church, while preserving the legacy of classical theology and philosophy, this encyclical rejected socialist solutions, criticized fiscalism (that is, government's use of its taxing and spending powers to shape the economy), and emphasized the significance of private property and free trade. Thus it approved the foundations of the capitalist system even while drawing attention to many essential corrections that it required. It also sketched a vision of society in which the state should play a crucial role but follow the principle of subsidiarity, supporting social activity as well as pluralism and a multitude of local, mediating associations.

QUADRAGESIMO ANNO

Without a doubt, the most important historical event accompanying the publication of Pope Pius XI's *Quadragesimo Anno* (The Fortieth Year) on May 15, 1931, was the Great Depression, which had begun in 1929. The worldwide depression had stunned people everywhere, resulting in bank closings,[20] spectacular suicides of stock market investors,[21] a catastrophic decrease in production,[22] and an astronomical rise in unemployment.[23] It laid bare the lack of effective legal regulation and the irresponsibility and corruption of those who ran the world's economy.

In this context, Pius's summary appraisal comes as no surprise: "All economic life has become tragically hard, inexorable, and cruel." The sources of this state of affairs were to be found, according to the pope, at the anthropological level—in individualism. Negating the social nature of ownership, and facilitating the separation of economics and ethics, individualism led to a threefold struggle: "First, there is the struggle for economic supremacy itself;

then there is the bitter fight to gain supremacy over the State in order to use in economic struggles its resources and authority; finally there is conflict between States themselves."[24] Unbridled free competition thus leads to the despotic rule of a plutocracy and permits the victory of the most ruthless of its representatives—it leads to suicide.

According to Pius, the philosophical setting that allowed these pathological developments in economic life was economic liberalism. Liberalism had shown itself "utterly unable to solve the social problem aright," which led to an idolatry of economic laws, reduced the role of the state to that of a "night watchman," secured privileges for those with capital (in accordance with the so-called Manchester School), and opposed labor unions.[25]

The pope's terminology is imprecise and hence subject to varied interpretations. From the context of *Quadragesimo Anno* one could conclude that Pius was concerned with extreme versions of classical liberalism that saw property rights as absolute and economic laws as impersonal and unchanging, analogous to the laws of physical science. These concepts, he observes, would be unfavorable to the state and negate the social nature of man. That the pope had ideological liberalism in mind—as a comprehensive vision of reality—is indicated by the encyclical's use of the phrase "idols of Liberalism."[26]

Several symptoms of social life confirmed the pope's appraisal. In the preceding years employers tended to receive more favorable treatment from governments than did employee organizations such as labor unions—a function often of a blind faith in the market and fear of state intervention, lack of antispeculative legislation and effective control, and the consolidation of immense power in the hands of economic dictators. Under such conditions, social injustice could flourish and the crisis could grow. On the other hand, the rise of monopolies and the concentration of economic power were mainly caused not by the *liberalization* but by the *politicization* of the economy. Furthermore, some of Pius's views (for example, regarding the Manchester School) were echoes of widely spread opinions rather than the result of analysis of primary-source materials.

Pius's critical opinion of the liberal order does not result in a more indulgent appraisal of socialism in *Quadragesimo Anno*. Far from it. The pope describes socialism as causing "extreme harm" to the working classes." Pius treats the two rival factions of socialism—communist and social democratic—not as two separate realities but as two pieces of one whole. Referring to the experience of the USSR, the pope concludes, "We, therefore, deem it superfluous to warn upright and faithful children of the Church regarding the impious and iniquitous character of Communism." He devotes much more attention to the "more moderate" form of socialism, which downplays the role of class conflict and the nationalization of property. The pope's message is explicit: he rejects any and all attempts to give socialism a Christian face—to "meet Socialism halfway, as it were." Pius concludes, "There are some allured by the foolish hope that socialists in this way will be drawn to us. A vain hope!"[27]

Explaining that man is endowed with a social nature to broadly develop his faculties and achieve temporal and eternal happiness, Pius writes that socialism, "wholly ignoring and indifferent to this sublime end of both man and society, affirms that human association has been instituted for the sake of material advantage alone." Such a pragmatic approach to society is connected in socialist thought with the need to socialize production. As a result, the pope writes, socialism requires people to "surrender and subject themselves entirely to society" with a view to the production of goods. This, in turn, leads to the claim that "the higher goods of man, liberty not excepted, must take a secondary place and even be sacrificed to the demands of the most efficient production of goods." Pragmatism as a social norm, the socialization of the individual, the deprivation of the individual's transcendence, and the slavery stemming therefrom are, according to Pius, inherent in socialist doctrine. This leads to the pope's unequivocal conclusion: "No one can be at the same time a good Catholic and a true socialist."[28]

Quadragesimo Anno's decisive criticism of both classical liberalism and socialism inevitably provokes the question of finding an intermediary solution—a third way. Pius, like Leo XIII before him, nostalgically recalls the guild system of the Middle Ages, and he appears more optimistic about adapting it to twentieth-century reality. This is why—standing face to face with the Great Depression and totalitarian Stalinist Russia, with unlimited free competition and individualism, on the one hand, and collectivism and central planning, on the other—the pope opts for a guild system that unites employers and employees in a collaboration for the common good. Pius regards with clear sympathy political attempts to reform a capitalism in deep crisis. Still, he notices the fundamental difference between the social life he postulates, based on freely created and autonomous fraternities, and the bureaucratic and political corporatism through which the state gains prerogatives for itself against the individual.[29]

Corporatism, broadly speaking, is a system of economic organization that sees the various bodies within society (for example, labor unions, firms, business groups), rather than individuals, as the main economic actors. It can take on a benign form that simply recognizes the importance of mediating institutions, or it can be manifested in a state-dominated economy that tramples on individual human rights. Pius's scholastic vision of society, the idealism characteristic of it (more easily seen from today's perspective), the frequent references to *Quadragesimo Anno* by Mussolini, Salazar, Franco, and the leaders of Latin American juntas—all helped to popularize a stereotype of Pius XI as the "father of corporatism." But the corporatism of fascist Italy was not the corporatism of the Roman pontiff. The term's equivocal meaning often disguises the economic and political foundations of the pope's proposed solutions.

From reading *Quadragesimo Anno* one might conclude that corporatism is, in essence, capitalism reformed through social justice and charity. For example, the pope calls for us to "restore society . . . on the firmly established basis of social justice and social charity." But one must keep in mind that Pius uses the term *society* in reference to capitalism as it actually existed. Recall that he rejects the alternatives: either completely unfettered competition or economic dictatorship. Pius claims that free competition is "justified and certainly useful provided it is kept within certain limits"; those limits require higher principles—the principles of social justice and charity.[30]

The German-Swiss economist Wilhelm Röpke rejected the idea that *Quadragesimo Anno* laid out a program of corporatism: "In each place where the 'ordines' [corporations, or professional communities] are mentioned and where their establishment is recommended, it is done simply with the social purpose of obtaining an improvement of the relations between employers and employees, that is to say, with the aim of dissipating the class struggle, and not of killing competition in the market." Röpke concluded, "I have been unable to find in the Encyclical any passage sanctioning the belief that an order based on the market economy should be replaced by another."[31]

Thorough analysis of the encyclical confirms this conclusion. Even in criticizing the economic system, Pius clearly states that "this system is not to be condemned in itself. And surely it is not of its own nature vicious." Problems occur, he explains, "when capital hires workers, that is, the non-owning working class, with a view to and under such terms that it directs business and even the whole economic system according to its own will and advantage, scorning the human dignity of the workers, the social character of economic activity and social justice itself, and the common good." Elsewhere, after analyzing the capitalist system, the pope describes the evolution of socialism, writing, "One section of Socialism has undergone almost the same change that the capitalistic economic system, as We have explained above, has undergone. It has sunk into Communism."[32] This means that the earlier critique of capitalism refers to its extreme and radical form; that critique therefore does not call for replacing capitalism with some new system of corporatism.

Pius explicitly endorses a market economy (properly regulated) as the path out of the Great Depression. The situation of the working class will improve, according to the pope, not simply through charity but also, and more important, through investments and the creation of abundant "opportunity for gainful work," which reflect the virtue of generosity. This whole description of economic life is characterized by realism. Pius notes, despite the crisis, the economic growth of the Western world and the betterment of the condition of the working class. To continue that growth and improvement requires the deproletarianization of laborers, which helps them advance themselves and democratizes property. Advising immediate reform, the pope nonetheless keeps economic reality in mind; he writes, for example, "Everyone knows that an excessive lowering of wages, or their increase beyond due measure, causes unemployment."[33]

Underscoring the fundamental meaning of the right to private property, Pius demonstrates the consistency of his attitude with the views of Leo XIII. But he explains, even more clearly than did his predecessor, the dual—individual and social—nature of ownership. He also reminds the reader of the universal destination of created goods, the moral truth that the resources of the world ought to benefit all of humanity, not only the fortunate few. Referring to *Rerum Novarum*, he recalls the difference between the right to ownership and the right to usage. Here, however, he adds that although the honest use of goods is a moral responsibility, it is false "to hold that a right to property is destroyed or lost by reason of abuse or non-use."[34]

Moreover, the pope criticizes statism. He maintains

that the state should be responsible for the legal regulation of a system of ownership that would take into account its dual nature, but it must not "discharge its duty arbitrarily." The state alone cannot create the conditions for economic and social growth. The problem, Pius suggests, is that the massive modern state has crowded out society's vital mediating institutions: "When we speak of the reform of institutions, the State comes chiefly to mind, not as if universal well-being were to be expected from its activity, but because things have come to such a pass through the evil of what we have termed 'individualism' that, following upon the overthrow and near extinction of that rich social life which was once highly developed through associations of various kinds, there remain virtually only individuals and the State."[35]

Once again Pius demonstrates the consistency of his views with Leo's. He recounts his predecessor's teachings on the subject of the right to free assembly and the right to choose the forms of association, and above all he strongly formulates the principle of subsidiarity, which he sees as "fixed and unshaken in social philosophy," a "most weighty principle" that cannot be set aside or changed." In other words, Pius explains, "Just as it is gravely wrong to take from individuals what they can accomplish by their own initiative and industry and give it to the community, so also it is an injustice and at the same time a grave evil and disturbance of right order to assign to a greater and higher association what lesser and subordinate organizations can do. For every social activity ought of its very nature to furnish help to the members of the body social, and never destroy and absorb them."[36] For Pius, then, the ideal is a decentralized state created by an active and self-organizing society, rich in social ties and independently undertaking the tasks standing before it.

By carefully examining the meaning of the words *liberalism* and *corporation* as the pope understood them, one sees that the vision of social life outlined in *Quadragesimo Anno*—in both its economic and political dimensions—clearly does not promote a corporatist third way or condemn liberalism.[37] Truer would be the opposite opinion, expressed by Röpke, one of the most distinguished representatives of the then-emerging "Ordoliberal" school (which gave rise to the German "economic miracle" after World War II): "Indeed, the 'liberal' quintessence of this document cannot be denied, so long as we take this word in its large and eternal sense of a civilization based on man and upon a healthy balance between the individual and community; so long, in short, as we accept liberalism as the antipodes of collectivism."[38]

Quadragesimo Anno sketches a vision of a capitalist system directed by social justice and charity, one in which property and the economy are democratized and the state is decentralized. In other words, the encyclical lays out the foundations of the form of politics and economics that would later be called "democratic capitalism."

MATER ET MAGISTRA

Thirty years after *Quadragesimo Anno,* and on the seventieth anniversary of the publication of *Rerum Novarum,* the social encyclical of Pope John XXIII analyzed social life in a manner more selective than that of his predecessors. As Oswald von Nell-Breuning, SJ, commented in October 1961, whereas *Quadragesimo Anno* contrasts a contemporary, disordered social climate with an immutable image of a healthy social order, *Mater et Magistra* (Mother and Teacher) concerns itself with capturing the latest tendencies in the development of social life in order to influence them. Such a perspective automatically creates difficulties in interpretation. The encyclical, in fact, has often been overinterpreted, treated as "leftist" or "rightist," "global" or "Eurocentric," "progressive" or "conservative," "avant-garde" or "supporting the status quo."

Czeslaw Strzeszewski is correct when he writes: "*Rerum Novarum* has been described as the encyclical on commutative justice, *Quadragesimo Anno* on social justice, and *Mater et Magistra* on distributive justice. The first of these primarily deals with the relationship of the employer to the employee, the second with the organization of social life from the perspective of the social good, and the last with the fair distribution of social income among social groups and world income among particular nations."[39] Yet as Michael Novak points out, *Mater et Magistra* includes new motifs, with John shifting away from the emphasis on distributive justice to what could be called "productive justice."[40]

This 1961 encyclical was written in the context of a postwar world experiencing dynamic changes. The pope writes, above all, about scientific and technical advancement. In the arena of social progress, he notes the development of insurance and other social welfare programs, the rise in education levels, the increase in prosperity, the broadened opportunity for advancement and the resulting decrease in class differences, and the growing awareness of the global dimension of social problems. The world was also witnessing political changes: ample access to public functions nearly independent of social and economic status, an increased sphere of state intervention, the decolonization of Asia and Africa, and an increase in international connections and, as a result, numerous associations and institutions of international scope.

From the point of view of our specific interest here, the first part of the encyclical takes on particular significance. It includes a series of weighty and explicit statements illustrating the principles of social life. "It should be stated at the outset," John writes, "that in the economic order first place must be given to the personal initiative of private citizens working either as individuals or in association with each other in various ways for the furtherance of common interests." The pope adds that state intervention is acceptable only if it leads to economic growth and, from there, to an advantage for all the citizens. Such intervention— which does the work of "directing, stimulating, co-ordinating, supplying and integrating" growth—must always be supported by the principle of subsidiarity. (Here the pope cites in full the formulation of this principle from *Quadragesimo Anno*.) John notes that governments could stimulate scientific and technical progress and thus help economic development, and that in recent decades they assumed more responsibility for controlling disturbances in the market and for the problem of mass unemployment. He argues that such protective government intervention must "never be exerted to the extent of depriving the individual citizen of his freedom of action"; instead, it must "augment his freedom while effectively guaranteeing the protection of his essential personal rights." John emphasizes this point when he adds, "Every economic system must permit and facilitate the free development of productive activity."[41]

The pope closes the discussion with the following deduction:

> Experience has shown that where personal initiative is lacking, political tyranny ensues and, in addition, economic stagnation in the production of a wide range of consumer goods and of services of the material and spiritual order—those, namely, which are in a great measure dependent upon the exercise and stimulus of individual creative talent.
>
> Where, on the other hand, the good offices of the State are lacking or deficient, incurable disorder ensues: in particular, the unscrupulous exploitation of the weak by the strong. For men of this stamp are always in evidence, and, like cockle among the wheat, thrive in every land.[42]

Here the pope closely connects respect for the right to private enterprise with respect for the right to private property. These two pillars of economic life constitute the capitalist economic system.

Specific comments in *Mater et Magistra*—for instance, statements supporting small and medium-sized properties; worker participation in management, in the profits and property of enterprises; and their representation in national and international institutions concerned with economic life—indicate that the pope's aim is to humanize work relationships and include workers in dynamic activities in the free market. In fact, John repeats the postulate of a radio speech Pope Pius XII gave in 1942, observing the "fundamental obligation of granting an opportunity to possess property to all if possible." He adds that "now, if ever, is the time to insist on a more widespread distribution of property" to guarantee freedom, support work effectiveness, protect the personal dignity of man, strengthen the family, and establish social peace.[43]

In stressing the advantages to be had from ownership of private property, John makes a discernible shift in accent. Whereas his predecessors claimed that private property is necessary for deproletarianization, as it stabilizes the material situation of the owner, John is pleased to note the development of social welfare. He writes:

> More and more people today, through belonging to insurance groups and systems of social security, find that they can face the future with confidence—the sort of confidence which formerly resulted from their possession of a certain amount of property.
>
> And another thing happening today is that people are aiming at proficiency in their trade or profession rather than the acquisition of private property. They think more highly of an income which derives from capital and the rights of capital.
>
> And this is as it should be. Work, which is the immediate expression of a human personality, must always be rated higher than the possession of external goods which of their very nature are merely

instrumental. This view of work is certainly an indication of an advance that has been made in our civilization.[44]

Hence deproletarianization is, in the words of the pope, less a matter of ownership than of creative human labor. If we connect this with his strong emphasis on private enterprise—his appreciation of the great role it plays in the production of material as well as spiritual goods, and in spurring innovation and economic development—we can argue that *Mater et Magistra* describes a system in which the individual, working creatively and in collaboration with others, functions within a free-market system based on the rules of private ownership. Michael Novak observes the pope's myriad comments regarding limiting the role of the state, noting that John stresses the many possibilities of human development and demonstrates the connection between freedom, self-realization, and responsibility. Novak calls this view "the pope's own liberal understanding" of society. He distinguishes it from the "liberal" view that the pope criticizes, while implying that John's concept of a just social order contains many "liberal" elements.[45]

One could agree with Novak's assessment, with a few reservations taken into account. First, John, acknowledging the primacy of the principle of subsidiarity, allows for and sometimes even recommends state intervention. Second, he strongly emphasizes the social function of private ownership. Third, he openly opposes all ideological forms of liberalism that separate ethics from economy, attempt to reconcile the laws of economy with the laws of nature, see profit and free competition as ends in themselves rather than as means to the common good, and accept no form of state intervention. Finally, the pope clearly indicates that all concepts of social order must be based on an integral concept of man. Novak admits this in the end. He cites the following fragment of the encyclical: "The cardinal point of [what the Catholic Church teaches and declares regarding the social life and relationships of men] is that individual men are necessarily the foundation, cause, and end of all social institutions. We are referring to human beings, insofar as they are social by nature, and raised to an order of existence that transcends and subdues nature."[46] Novak adds this commentary: "The first sentence sounds like the cardinal principle of liberalism. The second takes care to place it in the context of human social and transcendent nature. The cardinal tenet of liberalism is not so much denied as subsumed within a social and transcendent framework."[47]

If the description of economic life in *Mater et Magistra* matches the principles of a capitalist economy to some degree, the matter is more complex on the level of social philosophy. Some forms of liberalism are incompatible with John's views, but other forms (as Novak notes) may correspond to the papal vision.

John's treatment of communism and socialism is completely different from his handling of the liberal order. Contrary to some interpretations, the pope's terminology "*incrementum (progressus) rationum socialium*"—the development of social relations—means only the continually increasing number of interpersonal connections and rising interdependency among citizens.[48] According to the pope, this phenomenon carries both advantages and disadvantages. Certainly this term should not be translated as "socialization" in the usual sense of that word so as to support the conclusion that "having read *Mater et Magistra,* we cannot be sure that all forms of socialism, irrespective of its character, are forbidden to Christians."[49] Such a conclusion is all the more unfounded as John has clearly stressed "the fundamental opposition between Communism and Christianity" and stated that "no Catholic could subscribe even to moderate Socialism."[50]

This encyclical is, in fact, antistatist in its vision of society, but it is worth noting the selective approach to the subject. Perhaps because the "spirit of the times" favored the ideas of the political Left, statism, central planning, and socialism, *Mater et Magistra* speaks more positively of the state than did earlier encyclicals. One cannot help noticing statements expressing support for strong government intervention. For instance, the pope writes that the state should strongly influence the situation in agriculture via price regulation. The encyclical also includes these words: "It is therefore a great source of joy to Us to see those nations which enjoy a high degree of economic wealth helping the nations not so well provided."[51]

In a departure from *Quadragesimo Anno,* John does not repeat the warnings of Pius XI that wages that are too high cause unemployment. The clear admonitions of Leo XIII and Pius regarding excessive fiscalism become significantly weaker in John's writings. John writes, for example, "In a system of taxation based on justice and equity it is fundamental that the burdens be proportioned to the capacity of the people contributing." *Mater et Magistra* even suggests that farmers be favored in the structuring of tax policy.[52]

John also writes much regarding the weighty role of the state in planning. He does not clearly describe his position, however. The fact that he never explicitly opposes central planning permits a leftist commentator from *Esprit* to conclude: "We are already quite near the concept of planning. This concept, unfortunately, does not appear in the documents although the principle formulated there and the line of thinking outlined leads towards it."[53]

In light of the above, one could state that *Mater et Magistra*, while preserving the essence of the description of social life from *Rerum Novarum* and *Quadragesimo Anno*, is less balanced and, from an economic point of view, less realistic in its details.

PACEM IN TERRIS

Pope John XXIII published his second social encyclical, *Pacem in Terris* (Peace on Earth), in 1963. This encyclical was written in the context of continuing decolonization and rapid scientific-technical advancement, which contributed to optimism about the power of human civilization. Yet it was also written in the context of the erection of the Berlin Wall and the Cuban Missile Crisis, two political confrontations that threatened the outbreak of yet another global conflict. For these reasons, the encyclical is devoted to international problems. One can, however, find allusions and references to the problem of democracy and capitalism, which is our concern.

The key to John's thinking is personalism.[54] According to this view, the human being as person is the subject of universal and inalienable rights and responsibilities. This conviction implies that each human community should be constituted on the basis of respect for freedom and governed by the principle of subsidiarity.

The pope does not devote much space here to the economy. Among human rights in the economic sphere, he mentions the rights to work, to equitable conditions, to engage in economic activities, to fair family wages (though adapted to the capabilities of the economy), and to possess private property, which also entails social obligations.

Discussing the problem of aid to the poorest of countries, John appeals to "the more wealthy nations to render every kind of assistance to those States which are still in the process of economic development." He further demands that nations cooperate to facilitate the exchange of goods, capital, and people and suggests investment in the weakest economic regions. Hoping that these countries "in as short a time as possible attain to a degree of economic development that enables their citizens to live in conditions more in keeping with their human dignity," he warns that "they must be conscious that they are themselves playing the major role in their economic and social development; that they are themselves to shoulder the main burden of it."[55] Quite clearly, then, the pope emphasizes stimulation of economic growth over the redistribution of wealth.

Although John advises that "it is not possible to give a general ruling on the most suitable form of government," he affirms that the relations between governments and citizens, and between states, "must be regulated by the principle of freedom."[56] Among the human rights, John enumerates the basic ones applying to citizens: the right to form associations, to emigrate and immigrate, to play an active part in public life, and to enjoy the legal protection of one's rights.

Overall, *Pacem in Terris* rather clearly speaks in favor of a democratic, constitutional state of law. Notably, the pope closes his discussion of political power with a suggestion that democracy be generally recognized as a natural and positive political system: "The above teaching is consonant with any genuinely democratic form of government." Elsewhere he praises the three branches of government, which "afford sure protection to citizens, both in the safeguarding of their rights and in the fulfillment of their duties." He also recommends "constitutional procedures" that recognize individual rights and define the method by which public officials are selected and the ways in which they may exercise power.[57]

An essential change can be observed with regard to communism and socialism. First, the words themselves do not appear in the encyclical. Second, the pope—emphasizing that "it is always perfectly justifiable to distinguish between error as such and the person who falls into error," and that one should distinguish "a false philosophy of the nature, origin and purpose of men and the world" from "economic, social, cultural, and political undertakings"—accepts the possibility of cooperation between Catholics and the followers of such "false philosophies" in endeavors that are compatible with natural law or the teachings of the Church. John also writes about some people characterized by "generosity of spirit" who, having come into contact with injustice, "tackle the problem with such impetuosity that one would think they were embarking on some political revolution." The pope addresses the following message to these people: "If there is to be any improvement in human institutions, the work must be done slowly and deliberately from within."[58] Of course, the realities of socialism from East Germany to China, and of Marxist partisans in Asia, Africa, and Latin America, raise doubts as to the effectiveness of this argument.

A certain element of theoretical deliberation appears in the encyclical.[59] This is evident where the pope writes of human rights, counting among them the right to education, housing, health care, and social welfare in case of illness, old age, or accident. Whereas his predecessors emphasized the rights and freedoms of the "first generation" (that is, political and civic rights), John shifts the accent onto "second generation" rights (that is, social, economic, and cultural rights). The weakness of this sort of thinking lies in the fact that such rights do not easily translate into tangible forms of human assistance. Furthermore, the text of the encyclical does not suggest how these rights—encompassing each inhabitant of the planet—might be implemented, or the desired state of affairs at least approximated.

John does, however, closely link rights with responsibilities. Indeed, the chapter on human rights is followed by one on responsibilities, whose first subheading is "Reciprocity of Rights and Duties Between Persons."

POPULORUM PROGRESSIO

The social encyclical of Pope Paul VI, published in 1967, deals to a great degree with subjects discussed in *Mater et Magistra* and *Pacem in Terris*. *Populorum Progressio* (On the Development of Peoples) significantly differs from these two, however. This is owing—at least to some extent—to Paul's own intellectual education, as well as to changes in the group that prepared the draft of the document. As one commentator noted: "This encyclical is a French encyclical."[60]

Many authors criticized *Populorum Progressio* for confusing the issue, being unfamiliar with economic reality, and replacing the classical vision of the political-economic order with an ideological appraisal of reality.[61] Vincent Cosmao—in later years a well-known "liberation theologian"—responded to such critiques by saying that the new encyclical changed the level of discussion and dealt, above all, with the "theology of human progress." This, however, is not a strong argument. Compared with the other social encyclicals, *Populorum Progressio* does not seem essentially different in the theological perspective on social reality. In fact, one could say—looking at the later *Laborem Exercens*—that the theological perspective is more clearly present in other encyclicals than in *Populorum Progressio*. As Czeslaw Strzeszewski aptly observes, "Of the references mentioned in earlier documents St. Thomas Aquinas has disappeared completely; the Church Fathers so frequently cited in *Gaudium et Spes* [the Second Vatican Council's document "The Church in the Modern World"] have also disappeared; the number of references to the Holy Scriptures has decreased rather significantly; and a complete novelty is the citing of numerous ecclesiastical and secular authors."[62] Hence it is impossible to defend the thesis that Paul's encyclical displays an especially theological profile.

Regarding the vision of an political-economic order sketched on the pages of *Populorum Progressio*, it would be difficult not to agree with the leading ideologist of the Italian Communist Party in the 1960s, who wrote that this encyclical is innovative in that "the relation of private ownership of the means of production and natural law is set aside," and "the main villain, though with certain limitations, is no longer communism or socialism, but capitalism, colonialism, and the concept of liberalism which provided ideological justification of the capitalist reality."[63]

Indeed, the encyclical diagnoses the low awareness of the global character of social problems in some countries. It also provides a one-dimensional treatment of progress, understood solely as economic development. Moreover, discussions of a socioeconomic system are often abstract.

Only two paragraphs mention property, and both of them negatively. Paragraph 23 states that the right to private property is not absolute, and paragraph 24 says that "if certain landed estates impede the general prosperity . . . the common good sometimes demands their expropriation."

Even when the pope praises human invention and enterprise, he displays an ambivalent attitude toward work as such, treating it as a reality external and quasi-autonomous with respect to man. This perspective reflects a tendency to create generalizations insufficiently grounded in reality. Such generalizations are evident in the encyclical's approach to economic life: "Certain concepts have somehow arisen out of these new conditions and insinuated themselves into the fabric of human society. These concepts present profit as the chief spur to economic progress, free competition as the guiding norm of economics, and private ownership of the means of production as an absolute right, having no limits or concomitant social obligations. This unbridled liberalism paves the way for a particular type of tyranny, rightly condemned by Our predecessor, Pius XI, for it results in 'international imperialism of money.' "[64]

Michael Novak appropriately criticizes the lack of precision in these statements:

> The three terms which Paul VI singles out—*profit, competition,* and *property as an absolute right*—demand considerably more reflection than the one this encyclical offers. Is not profit another name for economic progress? A system producing no new wealth is either stagnant or declining. Is not competition better than state monopoly? Is not a universe of relatively self-reliant (although interdependent) states better than "international imperialism"? Did not John Locke, Adam Smith, and John Stuart Mill—and a host of other liberal thinkers—define private property through its service for the common good, and therefore as a *relative* right? Has not the history of liberal institutions in liberal societies been a history of growing checks upon the economic system, both through effective political reforms (such as the welfare state) and through free and critical moral-cultural institutions? Paul VI seems to assume that "liberalism" means only and solely a radical individualism, materialism, and Darwinian struggle.[65]

Paul is right to criticize the world for its egoism and insufficient sensitivity to the suffering of the poorest. But he criticizes the economic system *en bloc,* with no clearly defined limits, and thus his critique could extend to the very foundations of the free economy.

He fails to acknowledge, for instance, that property rights had not been seen as absolute in western European legislation since the nineteenth century. (The Napoleonic Code had, at the beginning of the nineteenth century, interpreted them in this way, but later civil law codes— German and Swiss—pointed out social limitations on property rights.) Also, labor and antitrust law had clearly outlined the direction taken by state intervention. Whereas the state had once regulated the economic sphere in accordance with the principle of unrestricted contracts, the developing field of labor law sometimes allowed the stronger side, the employer, to include clauses that were clearly disadvantageous to the employee. Furthermore, government was intervening in the market to ensure true and fair competition as capital was being concentrated and great monopolies were arising.

Paul admits, "Competition should not be eliminated from trade transactions, but it must be kept within limits so that it operates justly and fairly, and thus becomes truly human endeavor."[66] Nevertheless, he sharply criticizes the free-market economy, and as noted, he seems to question private property. In addition, he frequently portrays central planning as a panacea for the injustices of economic life.

The pope emphasizes that if our civilization is not regulated by some plan, then the disproportions between the wealthy and poor nations will continue to increase. He supports a convention on price regulation, appeals for a general plan for mutual assistance, obligatory for all nations, and a general fund to aid the poorest countries. Although he creates projects with concrete tasks, he gives no hints as to who would work out the details of the obligatory plan, nor which countries would pay into the fund and which would receive subsidies, nor according to what criteria sums would be paid in or out. The pope also suggests that money to assist the neediest nations could come from increased taxes or increased prices on imported goods.

To be sure, pleas to correct the existing system could be found in previous social encyclicals as well. Pius XI, for example, wrote positively of corporatism, and John XXIII proposed founding an international public authority. But—and this is in vivid contrast to *Populorum Progressio*—both emphasized that they were concerned with voluntary associations. Additionally, they displayed respect for freedom, property, and the principle of subsidiarity, themes barely touched in Paul's document.

Actual practice has demonstrated the ineffectiveness—indeed, the counterproductive nature—of the recipes proposed on the pages of *Populorum Progressio*. Real socialism, with its central planning, has been shown to be ineffective and to lead to corruption. This is another example of the lack of realism in the encyclical.

Many other examples can be found as well. For instance, the encyclical criticizes privileged prices for industrial goods with relation to foodstuffs as a cause of poverty in unindustrialized nations that export primarily agricultural products, but then, a moment later, the pope endorses agricultural subsidies in the developed countries, which artificially decrease prices on these crops. Paul also claims, "As a result of technical progress, the price of manufactured products is rising rapidly and they find a ready market."[67] In reality, as a result of technical progress, prices were *falling*. In the same paragraph, he states that the imbalance in wealth is rising because affluent countries sell industrial goods while the impoverished sell raw resources and agricultural goods.[68]

The words *socialism* and *communism* do not appear in *Populorum Progressio*. The encyclical only alludes to leftist ideologies when, for example, it praises the role of varied labor unions, the vast majority of which were closely linked with communist or socialist movements at that time. The famous reference to rebellions and uprisings—justifying revolution in cases of "manifest, longstanding tyranny"— is often misinterpreted as Paul's approval for revolutionary coups; actually, it recounts classical Catholic teaching, which permits rebellions and uprisings only in extreme cases.[69] Nonetheless, there again is the context: very sharp criticism of the contemporary world, directed mainly against liberalism and the wealthy nations. The lack of clearly defined limits to this criticism has enabled the encyclical to be interpreted in the spirit of Marxist liberation theology.

Laborem Exercens

The first social encyclical of John Paul II, 1981's *Laborem Exercens* (On Human Work), is above all a philosophical-theological treatise on man's labor. Only through such theological and philosophical discussions, conducted on their own level, do the papal opinions on social reality and practical solutions become manifest. These social and practical remarks are, nevertheless, always in the background and often innovative in their phrasing.

It is not easy to evaluate this document according to our criteria. If some commentators claim that *Laborem Exercens* is "a deep meditation and prophetic view,"[70] others argue that its realism is greater than that of all previous encyclicals.[71] A journalist from the *Spectator* of London wrote, "[*Laborem Exercens*] is so at variance with the laissez-faire 'New Jerusalem' Reaganites that one cannot ignore it. If the Pope were an American you would place him on the far left wing of the Democratic Party."[72] Simultaneously, the conservative, pro-Reagan Heritage Foundation published a book in which the author argued that *Laborem Exercens* constituted a great step forward in the evolution of Catholic social thought in the direction of democratic capitalism.[73]

This encyclical manifests the same social sensibility as *Populorum Progressio* and a similarly negative assessment of the contemporary world. Crucially, however, it shifts the accent by focusing on the concrete subject of human labor in its theological and philosophical aspect and by concentrating on the theme of the creatively active human being. An essential change that significantly influences the reading of this encyclical is that critical comments on capitalism and liberalism are accompanied by criticisms of socialism and communism. Moreover, John Paul clearly marks the difference between the Church's critical stances toward these social solutions. Recalling the teachings of the Church on private property (as well as the right to the means of production), the pope writes:

The above principle, as it was then stated and as is still taught by the Church, *diverges* radically from the program of *collectivism* as proclaimed by Marxism and put into practice in various countries in the decades following the time of Leo XIII's encyclical. At the same time, it differs from the program of *capitalism* practiced by liberalism and by the political systems inspired by it. In the latter case, the difference consists in the way the right to ownership or property is understood. Christian tradition has never upheld this right as absolute and untouchable.[74]

Later in the paragraph, the pope continues this line of thinking: "Therefore, while the position of 'rigid' capitalism must undergo continual revision, in order to be reformed from the point of view of human rights—both human rights in the widest sense and those linked with man's work—it must be stated that, from the same point of view, these many deeply desired reforms cannot be achieved by an *a priori elimination of private ownership of the means of production*."[75]

Another important difference from earlier social encyclicals is that John Paul defines the basic concepts. The pope's definition of capitalism is inspired by what happened in the early stages of capitalist development: he describes it as a system in which the person is treated as a tool of production, not as the creative subject of the discharged labor. He adds, "Precisely this reversal of order, whatever the program or name under which it occurs, should rightly be called 'capitalism.'" The pope also points out that "the error of early capitalism can be repeated wherever man is, in a way, treated on the same level as the whole complex of the material means of production, as an instrument."[76]

The second integral concept John Paul defines is economism: the ideology according to which human labor is treated as an exclusively economic category, thus eliminating any thinking about economic life in personal and humanist categories. Novak notes: "Economism is to the economy what scientism is to science."[77] Yet again the pope situates the error of economism in the early phases of capitalism, adding that it can be repeated anywhere.[78]

The next concept John Paul introduces is that of the "indirect employer," which "includes both persons and institutions of various kinds and also collective labor contracts and the *principles* of conduct which are laid down by these persons and institutions and which determine the whole socioeconomic *system* or are its result." The indirect employer, according to the encyclical, is responsible for conducting a labor policy—and it is, above all, the state that stands behind this: "The concept of the indirect employer is applicable to every society, but in the first place to the state."[79] Thus the pope makes the state coresponsible for the economy.

By defining fundamental ideas for the purposes of this document, John Paul avoids the ambiguities connected with their usage. Also more clearly delineated are the reasons why particular social, economic, and political solutions are praised or criticized.

In speaking of the role of the state, John Paul highlights the danger of statism, as Paul VI did not. He writes critically of the depersonalizing "system of excessive bureaucratic centralization." In speaking of comprehensive planning,

which is among the prerogatives of the indirect employer
and which should minimize the danger of unemployment,
he explains: "This overall concern weighs on the shoulders
of the State, but it cannot mean one-sided centralization by
the public authorities. Instead, what is in question is a just
and rational *coordination,* within the framework of which
the *initiative* of individuals, free groups, and local work
centers and complexes must be *safeguarded.*"[80] This right to
initiative is an outgrowth of the vision of man as a creative
subject, explicitly drawn on the pages of the encyclical.

This understanding of man informs the innovative
treatment of ownership in *Laborem Exercens.* The pope
considers the concrete forms of the right to ownership.
Recognizing the right to private property, he first notes that
"one cannot exclude the *socialization,* in suitable conditions, of certain means of production." Second, he emphasizes that "the position of 'rigid' capitalism continues to
remain unacceptable, namely the position that defends
the exclusive right to private ownership of the means of
production as an untouchable 'dogma' of economic life."
This is why reform is required, though not through the
elimination of private ownership. John Paul stresses that
socialization is possible only when "the subject character
of society is ensured, that is to say, when on the basis of his
work each person is fully entitled to consider himself as a
part-owner of the great workbench at which he is working
with everyone else."[81]

The pope views the problem of property from a perspective unique in the history of papal teaching. He recognizes the changing nature of property in an increasingly
technological world; no longer is land or even physical cap-

ital the dominant and ideal form of property. One dares to deduce that the concrete form property assumes is of little matter to John Paul, as long as it serves labor and protects the human subject. Early capitalism maintained the pre-eminence of property and its owner over labor, insofar as it was one economic factor, among others, of production. The worker received the material, and in transforming it, he in varying degrees appropriated the product, thanks to the change in value that his work created. According to a dynamic concept of property, it is not sufficient to take labor into account once the thing becomes a "product"; in the process of appropriation, one should value the work already transformed into matter. What makes something valuable and the essential reason for its appropriation depends on the knowledge and qualities brought to bear by the subject appropriating it. This is why things "cannot be *possessed against labor;* they cannot even be *possessed for possession's sake,*" but should serve labor.[82]

Personalism, which implies the dignity of man as the subject of labor, demands that this application of human effort and ingenuity becomes the source of the rights of the working individual. But the pope links these rights closely to the duty to work. Such rights and privileges include, according to John Paul, "suitable employment for all who are capable of it"; fair wages, by which the pope under-stands family wages; various social services ensuring the life and health of the worker; the right to rest; the right to assemble (the pope particularly emphasizes the role of labor unions but also warns against group and class ego-ism); and the right to emigrate.[83]

John Paul, starting from his own personalist view

of human life, delineates the basic and necessary circumstances that any fair and just system should fulfill.
Although it is not possible to describe unequivocally the
sociopolitical system the encyclical envisions, many critics
have convincingly argued that John Paul lends support to
democratic capitalism with his encyclical.[84]

SOLLICITUDO REI SOCIALIS

John Paul's second social encyclical, published in 1987, had
as its backdrop "the confrontation of two blocs, East and
West, and the threat of a nuclear war. Two themes are united
there and intersect in it: the defense of the dignity of the
human person by an equitable relation between work and
capital, and the anxiety of saving the peace." It was with
these words, written seven years after he penned *Sollicitudo
Rei Socialis* (On the Social Teaching of the Church), that the
pope himself characterized the context out of which that
encyclical emerged. *Sollicitudo Rei Socialis* only touches on
the theme that is the subject of analysis here, but one can
find in it new and weighty declarations.

John Paul, devoting his text mostly to the effects of
the ideological and military confrontation between the
East and West, writes that the former is inspired by Marxist collectivism and the latter by liberal capitalism. He
adds, "The Church's social doctrine adopts a critical attitude towards both liberal capitalism and Marxist collectivism."[85] From the context, this criticism seems to hinge
on the vast resources the confrontation between these
two systems has absorbed and on how, given the bilateral

character of the conflict, the needs of weaker nations were rarely taken into account (indeed, these nations were often treated instrumentally).

Despite the criticism of real capitalism and real socialism, the pope does not suggest seeking another political system. In fact, he opposes attempts to find an ideal system: "The Church well knows that no temporal achievement is to be identified with the Kingdom of God."[86] Of even greater significance is his unequivocal assertion that it is not for the social teaching of the Church to take up the construction of abstract theories; rather, he says, the Church should be engaged in evaluating reality in light of the Gospels. In other words, the pope expressly rejects thinking in categories of a third way in Catholic social thought. The encyclical states:

> The church's social doctrine is not a "third way" between liberal capitalism and Marxist collectivism, nor even a possible alternative to other solutions less radically opposed to one another: rather, it constitutes a category of its own. Nor is it an ideology, but rather the accurate formulation of the results of a careful reflection on the complex realities of human existence, in society and in the international order, in the light of faith and of the Church's Tradition. Its main aim is to interpret these realities, determining their conformity with or divergence from the lines of the Gospel teaching on man and his vocation, a vocation which is at once earthly and transcendent; its aim is thus to guide Christian behavior.[87]

This unambiguous wording, stressing the realistic nature of Catholic social thought, alters the meaning of the critiques made by its representatives. Such criticism does not aim to overthrow one social system and replace it with another that is optimal from a Christian point of view. Its goal turns out to be deciding whether and to what degree the existing social solutions are in accord with the teachings of the Gospel or whether they are capable of evolving in the spirit of those guidelines.

On the political and ideological level, one could perceive a certain symmetry in the pope's treatment of the West and the East.[88] According to this view, the encyclical portrays the two superpowers as pulling poorer and weaker states into a bilateral confrontation that precludes solutions to the problems facing the world. In other parts of the text, however, John Paul differentiates the accusations against the two global blocs.

The pope generally maintains that the source of injustice in the world is the craving solely for profits and for power "at any price," which builds "structures of sin." By using the term *structures of sin,* the pope challenges concepts of liberation theology, which employs the concept of "structural sin" to refer only to capitalism. That leftist theology thus speaks of an impersonal and genetic contamination of systemic solutions from the very outset. By contrast, John Paul immediately and strongly stresses that the "structures of sin" are always "rooted in personal sin, and thus always linked to the concrete acts of individuals who introduce these structures, consolidate them, and make them difficult to remove."[89]

Though the word *communism* is never mentioned in

Sollicitudo Rei Socialis, the pope criticizes its principles, political as well as economic. Calling for development in the contemporary world, John Paul stresses that certain "nations need to reform certain unjust structures, and in particular their political institutions, in order to replace corrupt, dictatorial and authoritarian forms of government by democratic and participatory ones."[90]

The pope clearly reproaches the system of real socialism in paragraph 15. Given the significance of this statement, it is worth quoting at length. After underscoring the meaning of the human right to private ownership, John Paul writes:

> Experience shows us that the denial of this right, or its limitation in the name of an alleged "equality" of everyone in society, diminishes, or in practice absolutely destroys the spirit of initiative, that is to say the creative subjectivity of the citizen. As a consequence, there arises, not so much a true equality, as a "leveling down." In the place of creative initiative there appears passivity, dependence and submission to the bureaucratic apparatus which, as the only "ordering" and "decision-making" body—if not also the "owner"—of the entire totality of goods and the means of production, puts everyone in a position of almost absolute dependence, which is similar to the traditional dependence of the worker-proletarian in capitalism. This provokes a sense of frustration or desperation and predisposes people to opt out of national life, impelling many to emigrate and also favoring a form of "psychological" emigration.

Such a situation has its consequences also from the point of view of the "rights of individual nations." In fact, it often happens that a nation is deprived of its subjectivity, that is to say the "sovereignty" which is its right, in its economic, political-social and in a certain way cultural significance, since in a national community all these dimensions of life are bound together.

It must also be restated that no social group, for example a political party, has the right to usurp the role of sole leader, since this brings about the destruction of the true subjectivity of society and of the individual citizens, as happens in every form of totalitarianism. In this situation the individual and the people become "objects," in spite of all declarations to the contrary and verbal assurances.[91]

This diagnosis decidedly rejects socialism. The encyclical declares that socialism's economic principles (nationalization of the means of production) and the foundations of national (monoparty system) and international politics (internationalism) harm not only the individual but the whole society.

The encyclical's criticism of "liberal capitalism" differs explicitly from that of "Marxist collectivism." The pope offers three serious objections: the idolatry of economic life, the promotion of a consumer culture, and an insufficient concern for the weakest. But these charges are not unique to liberal capitalism; they constitute a general critique of the condition of the contemporary world. In some cases the accusations refer as much to the "Socialist Bloc" as to Third World countries.

The pope warns against a deterministic treatment of economic processes that reduces the concept of "development" to economic growth and thus marginalizes other dimensions of human and social life—cultural, religious, and ethical. John Paul also criticizes consumerism or the "consumer society," "which easily makes people slaves of 'possession' and of immediate gratification, with no other horizon than the multiplication or continual replacement of the things already owned with others still better," and which often creates artificial needs.[92]

In writing of the poor, the pope stresses that the real responsibility for improving the fate of the poorest rests on the shoulders of the wealthier part of the world, regardless of any theories describing the current state of affairs. The moral challenge that cannot go unanswered is the dramatic situation of "real and unique persons, who are suffering under the intolerable burden of poverty." The pope faults the wealthy nations for insufficient aid to the poorest, for sometimes even taking advantage of their situation to increase profits (for example, giving credit with the stipulation that weapons be purchased from the creditor), and for subjecting poorer countries to inhumane provisos (for instance, making financial aid dependent on propagation of contraception). Significantly, however, John Paul departs from *Populorum Progressio* by emphasizing the responsibility of the poorest societies and governments themselves: "Development demands above all a spirit of initiative on the part of the countries which need it. Each of them must act in accordance with its own responsibilities, not expecting everything from the more favored countries."[93]

In short, it would be difficult to interpret John Paul's

criticisms of the contemporary world, which are particularly directed at the wealthier countries, as a general criticism of "liberal capitalism" or the systems reigning in Western nations. More precisely, his remarks could be described as a general critique applied to contemporary times, already outlined in *Laborem Exercens*—a criticism of economism as an ideology, with its practical materialism, idolatry of economic mechanisms, and egotistical individualism.

In fact, the pope offers several positive comments about the liberal institutions of democratic capitalism. In paragraph 44, he decisively speaks out for democracy. In paragraph 15, although he does not use the word *democracy*, he speaks out for a political system that respects the subjectivity of the citizen and society, while censuring any systems of guardianship.

On the subject of private ownership, the pope writes little, but his statement that "the right to private property is valid and necessary" is clear and straightforward. Nonetheless, John Paul stresses the principle of the universal destination of goods, stating this in terms heretofore not used in social encyclicals: "Private property, in fact, is under a 'social mortgage.' "[94]

To complete the picture, it should be added that the pope lists among human rights—and this is a novelty— *"the right of economic initiative,"* which he links with the common good. Moreover, the encyclical suggests that the poorest nations, to protect themselves from the monopolization of world markets, should expand cooperation and liberalize trade. John Paul clearly insists that political and economic life should be built on respect for freedom, solidarity, the subjectivity of man and society, and the participation of the greatest number of citizens. Essential here, too, is the pope's emphasis that man "was not created, so to speak, immobile and static."[95] Therefore, man is called to mature, grow, and develop—in the socioeconomic dimension as well.

Although John Paul criticizes ideological liberal capitalism and the numerous shortcomings to be found in the politics and economies of the West, he supports the institutions of democratic capitalism. As Michael Novak observes:

> He stands, fundamentally, as what Americans would call a "liberal," in at least three ways. Regarding the political order, John Paul asserts that democracy, the rule of law, limited government, and respect for human rights are "essential conditions" of a social order conformable to God's will. Regarding the economic order, the Pope emphasizes in a new way that "the right of economic initiative" is the fundamental principle of authentic development. This right springs from the image of God that inspires human subjectivity. Through it, humans are endowed by God with an inalienable creativity, which serves the common good of all. By the same token, all of creation is destined for the common good of all. Experience has shown that regimes of private property and private initiative better develop the resources of nature than do collectivist or traditionalist regimes, both of which are statist in different ways and degrees. As a limitation on the power of the state, the right to private initiative is necessary both for personal

creativity and for the common good. Regarding the moral order, the Pope makes religious freedom, pluralism, and the transcendent rights of conscience central to authentic development. The deprivation of such rights is worse than material deprivation. He says no scheme of development can justify imposing one's own faith or religion upon others. Where these moral criteria of John Paul II are given expression in the institutions of society, such a society would, in the honorific sense, properly be called a "free society." . . . *Sollicitudo Rei Socialis* does succeed in advancing Catholic social teaching beyond Paul VI in *Populorum Progressio,* and even beyond *Laborem Exercens.*[96]

Novak writes of the political, economic, and moral dimensions here; it would be worthwhile to pay particular attention to the anthropological one. From the vision of man—only sketched out on the pages of *Sollicitudo Rei Socialis,* which is devoted to another topic—an image emerges of a dynamic and creative individual actively participating in political and economic life. This is a fundamental difference from *Populorum Progressio,* from whose pages one could reconstruct the image of a person surrounded by a hostile and dominating environment.

From Rerum Novarum to Sollicitudo Rei Socialis

When one compares the social encyclicals written in the century after *Rerum Novarum,* it is possible to discern an

evolution in the Church's views on political-economic systems and in its postulated social solutions.

Such a comparison must be conducted very carefully,
however, since the authors of these encyclicals—even
of *Quadragesimo Anno*—never aspired to write a study
that would encompass the whole problem, and this lack
of a comprehensive solution inevitably opens the field to
deductive and inductive reasoning. The changing historical circumstances in which the subsequent documents
were published also broaden the field of interpretation. Yet
another crucial difficulty is the lack of precise or even consistent terminology from encyclical to encyclical.

Nevertheless, the *expressis verbis* opinions and empha-
ses placed on particular subjects allow us to reconstruct
a more general vision of economics and politics recorded
in the encyclicals. The first two documents offer a view
of political and economic life that corresponds with the
model of democratic capitalism. The following two pon-
tificates change this position, pulling away from—even
displaying some antagonism toward—the social solutions
of democratic capitalism. But Pope John Paul II curtails
this tendency, and in fact turns it around, in his first two
social encyclicals.

One can also see an essential shift in accent regarding the role of the state in social life. True, all the popes
oppose more extreme liberal, and especially libertarian,
concepts of the state and assign it a decisive role in social
life. But each encyclical treats the state's means as well as
its sphere of influence differently. The scholastic vision of
the state, a *societas perfecta* that was responsible for realizing the common good of all its citizens, is clearly present

not only in the encyclicals of Leo XIII—*Diuturnum Illud* (1881), *Immortale Dei* (1885), *Libertas Praestantissimum* (1888), and *Rerum Novarum* (1891)—but also in *Pacem in Terris* (1963), in the chapter titled "Relations Between Individuals and the Public Authorities within a Single State." Here John XXIII cites a radio speech in which Pius XII said that "it is from Him that State officials derive their dignity, for they share to some extent in the authority of God Himself."[97] In realizing this vision, the state should not only react in cases where the common good is transgressed but should also devote particular attention to the most impoverished strata of society. (Here the stress is less on direct aid and more on creating conditions to facilitate a better future.)

In practice, such a holistic view could easily lead to statism. Yet both Leo XIII and Pius XI provide counterbalance by underscoring the principle of subsidiarity, in which the role of the state is subservient and decentralized. Their encyclicals stress the primary role of the person in relation to the state. They also emphasize that a tight network of grassroots social ties—family and other mediating institutions—is a key source of the state's strength. In subsequent encyclicals, however, the role of civil society weakens as the popes evolve in the direction of the welfare state, attempting to ensure that each individual receives the largest possible packet of rights understood as privileges. The connection of these rights with corresponding responsibilities is evident in John XXIII, becomes practically imperceptible in Paul VI, but returns again in John Paul II.

Later encyclicals consistently bolster the role of the state in the international dimension. In the Church's view, states must be responsible for maintaining not only world peace but also international production, economic exchange, and assistance to the weakest nations. Still, over time the encyclicals shift on the question of whether nations that receive aid are responsible for wisely employing the assistance received and for their own development. John XXIII makes this point, but Paul VI deemphasizes it; John Paul II then reinstates it.

The problem of planning social development is, according to all the encyclicals, the prerogative of the state. Still, in *Populorum Progressio,* the planning and coordinating role of the state (present in earlier encyclicals) migrates in the direction of central planning of social life, and the field of intervention is greatly expanded. John Paul once again limits the meaning of central planning and this type of role for the state.

Discussion of specific political systems—especially of democracy, the form most essential to the work at hand—is barely present in the encyclicals. Leo did allow for a variety of systems (a novelty in those days) and dislodged the odium weighing on this idea since the times of the French Revolution. A crucial change took place during World War II, when the experience of totalitarianism pushed Pius into making positive reference to democracy. John XXIII took up the thinking of his predecessor, and the Second Vatican Council developed it further. Once again, this is indiscernible in Paul VI but returns as a strengthened antitotalitarian theme in John Paul II.

Over time, too, the encyclicals display evolving attitudes toward capitalism (and classical liberalism) and toward socialism (and communism). Leo and Pius take an approving but critical stance on capitalism, which stands in stark contrast to their unequivocally negative attitude toward socialism. The dissimilarity definitely decreases in John's and Paul's writings: the critique of socialism appears to be even more moderate than that of capitalism. The situation changes again in John Paul's encyclicals, demonstrating that the practice of real socialism is significantly more discordant with the Church's social teachings than is capitalism.

The Church's views on capitalism and socialism inform the shift in attitudes toward a third way—an alternative Christian model of social life. Leo and Pius evince a theoretical desire for real capitalism to model itself on the medieval guild system of corporations. In John's texts one can discern a model built on neither past nor present projects (that is, not counting the general idea of world government). Paul does not construct any theoretical scheme, although he positively appraises socialism's institutions while censuring capitalism, in practice as well as in theory. Such strong criticism makes thinking about a third way inevitable, and one could assume that more solutions could be drawn from socialism than from capitalism. John Paul, however, rejects the very idea of constructing a third way.

Another clear evolution occurs in the popes' attitudes toward economic life—private and public property, open competition and central planning, fiscalism, and production and distribution. Especially if we add to our discussion the teachings of Pius XII (contained in various addresses and encyclicals that do not focus specifically on social issues), the Second Vatican Council's *Gaudium et*

Spes, and Pope Paul VI's 1971 apostolic letter, *Octogesima Adveniens,* it is easy to discern a migration from solutions and institutions traditionally connected with capitalism toward solutions connected with socialism. With regard to the essential issue of private property, a pivotal change takes place during the course of John XXIII's pontificate. Until that time, popes had spoken decidedly in favor of the institution of private property. John did likewise in *Mater et Magistra;* he even entitled one of its subchapters "Confirmation of the Right of Private Property." *Pacem in Terris* includes significantly fewer mentions of ownership but still stresses that the right to property is inherent in human nature. *Gaudium et Spes* does similarly. In *Populorum Progressio,* however, private property is described rather negatively, and in *Laborem Exercens,* neutrally, as one of several forms possible. *Sollicitudo Rei Socialis* finally brings a reserved but positive comment that this privilege is "valid and necessary."[98] At the same time, from Leo XIII to John Paul II, popes have increasingly emphasized the social dimension of ownership, as stemming from the universal destination of created goods.

This brief review of the social encyclicals from *Rerum Novarum* to *Sollicitudo Rei Socialis* illustrates an essential evolution in the Church's social thought regarding economic and political systems. Part of this evolution reflected changing social reality. Robert Royal raises this important consideration as he analyzes the language of *Populorum Progressio:* "In this as in many of the last papal documents, *la question du style* is not without meaning. In *Rerum Novarum* (1891) and *Quadragesimo Anno* (1931), the two cornerstones of modern Catholic social teaching, the language is crisp in a way that is largely absent in the later encyclicals. The drafters of the earlier texts were particularly careful because they thought someone might, at some point, ask them to form a government on their principles. Subsequent encyclicals, with no such possibility in view, exhibit a corresponding lack of meticulous attention to social problems. In the later texts, genuine moral urgency frequently jumps to quick political conclusions or even outright simplifications of complex social realities."[99]

Such simplifications would be less evident in *Centesimus Annus* (Hundredth Year), Pope John Paul II's social encyclical issued exactly a century after *Rerum Novarum*. At the threshold of a new millennium, *Centesimus Annus* would introduce important new elements in the Church's social teaching and assume the role of the flagship of Catholic social doctrine. Any consideration of the Church's teaching on democratic capitalism must pay special attention to *Centesimus Annus,* which is why this comprehensive encyclical is the subject of the chapters that follow.

POLITICAL COMMUNITY

The encyclical *Centesimus Annus* was, above all, Pope John Paul II's response to the fall of the Communist system—a feat achieved in great measure thanks to him—as well as his counsel on the building of a new social order after the end of the Cold War.[1] The pope devotes two out of six chapters to reflections on these events. Subsequent chapters include recommendations regarding the forms of socioeconomic life that could be adopted by the nation-states that recovered their independence after 1989.

Centesimus Annus, issued on May 15, 1991—the hundredth anniversary of *Rerum Novarum*—is undoubtedly inscribed in that register of Roman Catholic social thought best represented by *Rerum Novarum* and *Quadragesimo Anno*, sketching the comprehensive and balanced contours of a socioeconomic system. Yet it is not only a modern link to the foundations of the Church's social thinking; it is also an innovative document.[2] In effect, the encyclical clarifies the Church's position on democracy and capitalism, a position appreciably more favorable than that of *Rerum Novarum* and *Quadragesimo Anno*. It introduces a distinction between faith and ideology, drawing important conclusions for the Church and the world. The encyclical also depicts anew the relationships between society and the state, and, more clearly than any such previous document, it demonstrates the preeminence of culture and anthropology over politics and economics.

From this point of view, *Centesimus Annus* represents the new language of the Church in its dialogue with the world. As such, it deserves searching analysis.

FREEDOM AND TRUTH

To reconstruct the papal vision outlined on the pages of *Centesimus Annus*, we must consider the encyclical's key themes: political community, economic life, and the primacy of culture. This chapter examines the first of these, political community, which involves the foundations of social life and the role of the state.

To begin with, *Centesimus Annus* makes some important assertions about the Church's attitude toward the world. John Paul writes that "the Christian faith does not presume to imprison changing sociopolitical realities in a rigid schema, and it recognizes that human life is realized in history in conditions that are diverse and imperfect." That is why "the Church has no models to present; models that are real and truly effective can only arise within the framework of different historical situations, through the efforts of all those who responsibly confront concrete problems in all their social, economic, political and cultural aspects, as these interact with one another."[3] This pluralistic response maintains the traditional position of Christian thought concerning the Church's independence from any particular form of government,[4] which underscores the Church's metapolitical mission. Any note of nostalgic longing for old systemic forms is absent, as is any desire to construct some optimal social solution. More to the point, the goal of the Church's social teachings—here John Paul stresses a thesis first set forth in *Sollicitudo Rei Socialis*—is not to promote a "third way" between concurrent models of sociopolitical life.

Other statements reinforce the pope's antimodel stance. "No political society—which possesses its own autonomy and laws—can ever be confused with the Kingdom of God," the encyclical states. Further on, John Paul writes, "Temporal societies . . . as the adjective indicates, belong to the realm of time, with all that this implies of imperfection and impermanence." The unavoidable multitude of possible systems (derived from different, ultimately theological, premises about the nature and end of man), the structural imperfection, and the transience of all social solutions mean that community life should be characterized by meliorism—the gradual perfection of existing structures and institutions: "In union with all people of good will, Christians, especially the laity, are called to this task of imbuing human realities with the Gospel."[5]

Meliorism is not the same as utopianism. Emphasizing the distinction between human political society and the

Kingdom of God, John Paul explicitly warns—and this is a significant theme in his teachings—against a utopian faith in an ideal solution, which can lead to terror and totalitarianism in social life: "When people think they possess the secret of a perfect social organization which makes evil impossible, they also think that they can use any means, including violence and deceit, in order to bring that organization into being. Politics then becomes a 'secular religion.'" As a Polish commentator rightly observed, "This encyclical shows how very complex human reality is. This complexity is what calls for the open, humble, and prudent attitude of which the Pope sets an example, precisely because he is drawing on the revealed truth about man."[6]

One essential point often passes unnoticed: John Paul's antiholistic and antitotalitarian position is, to a great extent, in accord with the views of distinguished representatives of classical liberal thought—figures like F. A. Hayek, Milton Friedman, and Karl Popper, all of whom criticized the sweeping social visions that in extreme form led to totalitarianism.[7] Nevertheless, there is a fundamental difference between the pope and these thinkers. The latter situate religion—marked, by its nature, with the conception of absolute truth—in the category of humanly constructed answers, which inevitably cause social life to fall under totalitarianism. Hence John Paul performs a great service—and introduces a novelty in the Church's social thinking—by accentuating the distinction between Christianity and ideology:

Nor does the Church close her eyes to the danger of fanaticism or fundamentalism among those who, in the name of an ideology which purports to be scientific or religious, claim the right to impose on others their own concept of what is true and good. *Christian truth* is not of this kind. Since it is not an ideology, the Christian faith does not presume to imprison changing sociopolitical realities in a rigid schema, and it recognizes that human life is realized in history in conditions that are diverse and imperfect. Furthermore, in constantly reaffirming the transcendent dignity of the person, the Church's method is always that of respect for freedom.[8]

By the encyclical's account, ideology maintains a concept of truth and goodness that captures all of reality in a simple and solid schema, and its advocates believe that this concept can be imposed on other people.[9] Christian truth, the pope observes, does not fulfill this second condition and therefore is not an ideology.

The Christian attitude of humility toward truth is fundamental in this context. Ideologues and their followers claim not only that they have grasped the objective truth that clarifies the essence of reality but also that they know this truth so well that they can impose their vision on the rest of society—that is, on people who for some reason (whether class, race, intellectual capacity, sin, caste, nationality, or religion) are incapable of perceiving it.

Ideologues' conviction of *truth possession* does not, however, necessarily stem from a belief in the *existence of an absolute truth*. When John Paul claims in *Centesimus Annus* that Christian truth is not an ideological truth, he is trying to say much more than the fact that the Church well understands that the complex political and economic reality cannot be captured in simple and brittle formulas. He is also trying to say something more than the fact that the Church stands against using a position of power to impose its concept of the truth and the good (although this has sometimes occurred in its history). In writing of the nature of Christian truth, the pope is stepping onto the theological plane. Christian truth is fundamentally different from ideological truth in that it does not allow itself, by its very constitution, to be possessed by any human being. Any ideology growing out of the Christian subsoil, even if it calls itself the quintessence of Christian engagement or orthodoxy, does not constitute an integral and consistent profession of Catholic faith; on the contrary, it always constitutes an abuse of the truth and a falsified version of Catholicism.

Christian truth has a dialectical character. It is indeed absolute and revealed to the Church, but the Church is not its owner, only its depository.[10] This truth surpasses the Church, for truth is situated beyond the human, the rational, the philosophical, and the theological. Only God Himself can be the sole possessor of the truth. As theologian Hans Urs von Balthasar put it, "This incomprehensible love of the God who acts in the event of Christ raises him far above all the incomprehensibilities of philosophical notions of God which consist simply in negating all statements about God, which may be ventured on the grounds of our knowledge of the world, out of regard for his total otherness."[11] St. Augustine himself wrote of "the truth, from whose transparent clarity our faith is as far removed as mortality is from eternity."[12] In yet another place in *De Trinitate*, he explained, "The certitude of knowledge will not be completed until after this life when we see face to face (1 Cor. 13:12). Let this then be what we set our minds on, to know that a disposition to look for the truth is safer than one to presuppose that we know what is in fact unknown."[13]

Divine truth was granted to the Church and then sufficiently comprehended by it so as to lead people to salvation. But in fixing certain principles regarding social reality, this truth by no means contains a ready project for social life or a political-economic system. Because divine truth, of its very essence, transcends the Church, one of the Church's most important tasks is to protect it from being locked into purely human categories.[14]

This humility toward a truth that transcends every man and the whole Church enables a critical approach toward ideologies. Cardinal Walter Kasper develops the thought with great acumen:

> The option for meaning that is made in faith in God proves itself adequate to our experience of reality by virtue of the fact that since it is a pre-apprehension of irreducible mystery, it cannot claim to be a complete explanation of reality and all its phenomena. On the contrary, the option for meaning that is present in faith is supremely critical of any total explanation of the world. This option brings with it a decided capacity for being critical of ideologies, because it points beyond all absolutizations of finite values—possessions, power, pleasure, honor, or nation, race, or class to an ever greater freedom,

and thus constantly makes us free and keeps history open-ended. It has not only an affirmative function but a critical one as well. . . . It has no need of putting on ideological blinders and of reducing the many-leveled and ambiguous whole of reality to a single dimension, be this the dimension of the positivist or the spiritualist, the pessimist or the optimist.[15]

Kasper stresses something extremely important here: that a conscious faith can never provide an exhaustive explanation of reality, and thus there is an immanent tendency to de-ideologize all systems and values. In other words, the divine truth cannot, without serious injury to itself, become a hermetic concept of the truth and of the good; it has by nature an anti-ideological character. Similarly, the certainty, stemming from the truth of original sin, that the Kingdom of God cannot be built on Earth also implies the antimodel nature of Catholic social thought.

It is impossible to overlook the basic problem that, for non-Christians, a theological argument evincing the unique character of Christian truth may prove incomprehensible, or at least unconvincing. Indeed, history seems to show that, despite the undeviating nature of divine truth, this truth has sometimes been interpreted differently in the past; worse, the Catholic religion has acted cruelly in defense of the truth, taking on the form of an ideology. The Second Vatican Council, while not raising the subject of ideology explicitly, clearly addressed dangers to human freedom in *Dignitatis Humanae*, the Declaration on Religious Freedom. The council declared that "truth can impose itself on the mind of man only in virtue of its own truth." Moreover, on the basis of natural law, each person has the right to freedom from physical and psychological coercion. This right is inviolable, as "the right to this immunity continues to exist even in those who do not live up to their obligation of seeking the truth and adhering to it."[16] The nonideological character of the Church's activity in the world thus flows from a theological reflection on truth and liberty and from a recognition of the dignity of each man. It is not faith but ideology that can easily be lured toward totalitarian solutions, since only the followers of the latter are convinced that they possess the solution for arriving at the best form of social system.

This does not mean—let us underline it once more—that religious faith is not threatened by the temptation of ideology, which appropriates truth and reduces faith to the level of a system of ideas. John Paul was conscious of this danger. He clearly expressed the problem in his warning, quoted above, about "the danger of fanaticism or fundamentalism" among those seeking "to impose on others their own concept of what is true and good." Several other comments in *Centesimus Annus* reinforce the point. The pope writes, for example, of the chimeras of Marxism, the risks and perils of a certain kind of capitalism, the oppression exercised by dictators (which consequently motivates the oppressed to free themselves), and aggressive forms taken by religious fundamentalism. In short, all forms of ideology are to be denounced. As for the Christian truth, outside the Church as well as in its bosom, it purifies; it unmasks and relativizes all conceptions of the social life that await the "end of history."

In this way the Church discharges the role of guardian of freedom in society. Cardinal Joseph Ratzinger, who would become Pope Benedict XVI, described this role more precisely:

> It is only where the duality of Church and state, of the sacral and the political authority, remains maintained in some form or another that the fundamental pre-condition exists for freedom. Where the Church itself becomes the state freedom becomes lost. But also when the Church is done away with as a public and publicly relevant authority, then too freedom is extinguished, because there the state once again claims completely for itself the justification of morality; in the profane post-Christian world it does not admittedly do this in the form of a sacral authority but as an ideological authority—that means that the state becomes the party, and since there can no longer be any other authority of the same rank it once again becomes total itself. The ideological state is totalitarian; it must become ideological if it is not balanced by a free but publicly recognized authority of conscience. When this kind of duality does not exist the totalitarian system is unavoidable.[17]

SOCIETY

In *Centesimus Annus*, John Paul II presents a classical vision of the Church's social teachings. This vision is based on two pillars of belief about human beings: they are persons, and they possess a social nature. As such, the encyclical criticizes proposals for "thoroughgoing individualism." Such proposals lead people to regard their lives as merely a "series of sensations to be experienced rather than as a work to be accomplished." According to the individualist perspective, man becomes "more like a producer or consumer of goods" than a subject, a *person*, who produces and consumes.[18] Equally misguided, the encyclical warns, are solutions that "socialize" man; these approaches fail to see him a person, that is, as an autonomous subject endowed with transcendent dignity, reason, and liberty.

From this vision of man, John Paul introduces the concept of the "personality (or subjectivity) of society," discussing the distinction between the "body politic" (or "political society," to use Catholic philosopher Jacques Maritain's terminology) and the state.[19] The pope understands that various social groups must be autonomous with respect to the state, that self-organizing, mediating institutions of society are necessary for the preservation of liberty. As Juan-Miguel Garrigues remarked, "Without intermediate bodies, there is no free society."[20] John Paul notes that these mediating communities "give life to specific networks of solidarity . . . and strengthen the social fabric, preventing society from becoming an anonymous and impersonal mass." The ideal is a robust society, interconnected by numerous interpersonal ties and organized at a grassroots level. "It is in interrelationships on many levels that a person lives, and that society becomes more 'personalized,'" he concludes, clearly referring back to the social vision outlined in *Rerum Novarum* and *Quadragesimo Anno*.[21]

It is easy to discern in this vision of the self-organizing society a convergence with the liberal tradition, especially its Anglo-Saxon variety. As Pierre Manent wrote in
his classic treatise on the subject, *An Intellectual History of
Liberalism*, "The foundation of liberalism is the distinction
between civil society and the state: the latter is the representative instrument of the former. Civil society tends to
be self-sufficient."[22] But most contemporary theorists deal
primarily with making sound social contracts and setting
the democratic rules of the game and procedures; they take
care to avoid deliberations on the nature of man and the
ends of life in society,[23] as these would encroach on the liberal principles of equality and neutrality. John Paul does
not similarly shy away from the discussion; he goes on to
treat the alienation of man and of society.

At the outset, the pope notes that the Marxist concept
of alienation, limited to "the sphere of relationships of production and ownership," is "mistaken and inadequate." It
is mistaken because it denies "the legitimacy and positive
value of market relationships." The Marxist concept has
been tested in practice—and proved false by the "historical experience of socialist countries."[24]

The Marxist concept is inadequate because it reduces
alienation to a purely materialistic level. For John Paul,
alienation has an even deeper and more universal nature. It
is evident even in prosperous Western liberal democracies.
Alienation appears in "consumerism," when man becomes
entangled "in a web of false and superficial gratifications,"
or when the work world is "organized so as to ensure
maximum returns and profits with no concern whether
the worker, through his own labor, grows or diminishes

as a person." The pope describes the essence of alienation: "When man does not recognize in himself and in others the value and grandeur of the human person, he effectively deprives himself of the possibility of benefiting from his humanity and of entering into that relationship of solidarity and communion with others for which God created him. Indeed it is through the free gift of self that one truly finds oneself."[25]

"False consciousness," bringing about the alienation of man, is caused by the weakening, or sometimes even the disappearance, of the transcendent dimension and of the sentiment of solidarity in the subject who seeks to understand himself. With this diagnosis, John Paul moves beyond what marks the limits of the liberal horizon: equality, justice (understood in a legalistic way), and the market. These phenomena are, to be sure, necessary for the existence of the human community. But a society constituted solely on this basis would be a dehumanized society. For example, even while praising the free market as "the most effective instrument for utilizing resources and effectively responding to needs,"[26] the pope notes that it effaces, in a structural way, the personal dimension of man, by treating him as a consumer or producer. Justice, too, deals with individuals rather than *persons*. And there are huge areas of social life—and still more of private life—within which the calculus of equality cannot rule. Everything associated with the love of the family, of the neighbor (above all solidarity with the sick, the disabled, the elderly, children, and the poor), or of one's country is more appropriately understood by the logic of the gift.

There also remain spheres of social life that, despite

their presence in the free market, cannot, given their fundamentally personal dimension, be treated as exclusively free-market territory. This includes the labor market. Human labor is so closely connected with the person that treating it merely as the object of a "buy-sell" contract would reduce man himself to a thing to be bought and sold. "In effect," John Paul writes, "beyond the rights which man acquires by his own work, there exist rights which do not correspond to any work he performs, but which flow from his essential dignity as a person."[27] Scholar and politician Rocco Buttiglione comments, "Therefore society appears divided into two spheres which remain in liaison with one another, but are nevertheless disconnected. One of them is the market. The second is the set of activities capable of responding to the needs which appear outside the market and most of which can be satisfied only according to the rules of gratuity."[28]

Fundamentally important for the very existence of a society is whether social life recognizes both of these spheres or, still more, whether it strengthens and supports the sphere of disinterestedness. The religion and culture within which a person lives and develops, along with customs, norms, and education, can determine whether he discovers the transcendent dignity of each individual and realizes his humanity by giving himself to others. Thus, according to John Paul, "A society is alienated if its forms of social organization, production and consumption make it more difficult to offer this gift of self and to establish this solidarity between people."[29]

Critics of this position could say that it is too idealistic, since human cooperation cannot be based on promoting the logic of the gift. In the past it has been more realistic to organize social life according to rationally defined personal interests and accept conflict in the life of a political community as inevitable. Critics could also assert that John Paul's position is antipluralistic because it is based on a specific way of understanding positive liberty. Thus, despite its noble motivations, if it were to take on a social dimension it could become an ideology and lead to totalitarian solutions.

But an attentive reading of *Centesimus Annus* demonstrates that John Paul's views on the alienation of man and society do not invalidate the encyclical's pluralistic, anti-utopian, and anti-ideological character. An ideal vision of social life as harmonious and exempt from conflict does not flow from the Church's doctrine. The Church recognizes that because of original sin, conflict is an indelible part of human history. At several points in *Centesimus Annus* the pope notes that social conflict is inevitable. Citing *Laborem Exercens* and *Quadragesimo Anno*, he even observes that conflict can have a positive role: as long as hatred and violence are absent, conflict and struggle can contribute to the construction of a better world.

But if we do not see social conflicts as evil, and instead accept them as a natural element of social life, then we risk losing the motivation to make a consistent and concerted effort to overcome them. At the same time, if we neglect the principles of the common good and solidarity, "conflict is not restrained by ethical or juridical considerations, or by respect for the dignity of others (and consequently of oneself)." We then treat social life as a useful space for attaining particular advantages, or even for unbridled rivalry, "transferring to the sphere of internal conflict between social groups the doctrine of 'total war.'"[30]

According to John Paul, the totalitarian ideologies lead to such radical conflict. But the liberal version of society can lead to strong antagonisms as well. With its rationalism and unmeasured optimism, it is blind to the sinister logic of the escalation of contradictions, of resentments and of accumulated prejudices between antagonists, of the spirit of revenge and of the human propensity to do evil.

Likewise, promoting one's own interests is nothing reprehensible as long as these interests are formed and limited by religion, ethics, and culture and do not break with the common good. Man can, in this sense, "transcend his immediate interest and still remain bound to it." John Paul notes that "the social order will be all the more stable" if it "does not place in opposition personal interest and the interests of society as a whole, but rather seeks ways to bring them into fruitful harmony."

Of course, man also "bears within himself the wound of original sin, which constantly draws him towards evil and puts him in need of redemption." Therefore a rational individual interest cannot suffice to build a vibrant, unified society. It will change into a shallowly understood egoism, transmitting a fatal germ into the collective life. The solution is not to deny the existence of egoism or to ignore it; instead it is to maintain strong ethical foundations and social mechanisms that limit egoism, to strengthen the sense of the common good, and to uphold religious and cultural premises that promote the logic of the gift of self. That is why it is so important to actually discern the problem of alienation. According to John Paul, the alienation of the person and of society withers the bonds between persons, which only encourages separatist attitudes and conflicts. Overcoming this alienation is therefore essential for the life of a society.

Many people outside the Catholic Church—particularly those who have eliminated from their deliberations the problems of the nature of man and of his vocation, of good and evil, and of egoism and love—may regard John Paul's arguments as little more than an attempt to impose a confessional ideology on our modern pluralistic civilization. Here it is important to remember that the necessary condition for a rapprochement of individual and society is respect for the liberty of the person. The pope states, "Indeed, it is through the free gift of self that one truly finds oneself." Hence one cannot force another to make this gift. Elsewhere the pope develops this thought: "Not only is it wrong from the ethical point of view to disregard human nature, which is made for freedom, but in practice it is impossible to do so. Where society is so organized as to reduce arbitrarily or even suppress the sphere in which freedom is legitimately exercised, the result is that the life of society becomes progressively disorganized and goes into decline."[31]

The respect for human liberty as a foundation of life in society is a leitmotif of *Centesimus Annus*. The encyclical offers a vision of what can be called an open society, at the heart of which is respect for individual liberty and for the liberty of the family and other social units. The emphasis is on building and consolidating bonds with other people. The pope writes, "Man remains above all a being who seeks the truth and strives to live in that truth, deepening his understanding of it through a dialogue which involves past and future generations." Further, "From this open search for truth, which is renewed in every generation, *the culture of a nation* derives its character." John Paul also stresses the failings of the isolationist stance, both in the economic and cultural sense: "When a culture becomes inward-looking, and tries to perpetuate obsolete ways of living by rejecting any exchange or debate with regard to the truth about man, then it becomes sterile and is heading for decadence."[32]

STATE

In *Centesimus Annus*, the principles ruling life in society also determine the role of the state, the basic political structure that gives form to social reality. John Paul, while recounting the traditional Catholic teaching of the primacy of man with respect to the state, which Leo XIII had maintained in *Rerum Novarum*, goes far beyond his predecessors' thinking about the state. Whereas previous popes had erected divine authority as a model for state institutions, John Paul, chastened by the experience of totalitarianism, emphasizes the need for limits on state power.

In their ascent toward omnipotence, states, especially authoritarian ones, habitually abused the idea that the institution of power comes from God. As philosopher of law Russell Hittinger points out, John Paul makes an important departure when he leaves behind his predecessors' philosophical approach of the divinely inspired *civitas*. Hittinger writes, "*Centesimus Annus* does not reflect the elegant metaphysical scheme of *Rerum Novarum*. Nor does it maintain the scholastic language that shaped the thought of both conservative and progressive pontiffs over the past century." John Paul's view of the political state aligns more closely with the modern notion of liberal political and legal institutions.[33]

Without a doubt, John Paul's view of the state was significantly influenced by the destructive force of ideological regimes in the twentieth century. This is reflected in the encyclical's critical comments on contemporary totalitarianism and authoritarianism, as well as nationalism and religious fundamentalism. John Paul veers away from a certain acceptance of state control of society, an idea well represented in the Catholic social teaching of previous decades (as we saw in chapter 1). Indeed, the pope distances himself overtly from the providential state, the state as dispenser of well-being—that is, the *welfare state.* "By intervening directly and depriving society of its responsibility," the encyclical states, "the Social Assistance State leads to a loss of human energies and an inordinate increase of public agencies, which are dominated more by bureaucratic ways of thinking than by concern for serving their clients."[34] The pope emphasizes that state interventionism stifles civic initiative and enterprise and makes citizens dependent on the state.[35] State assistance is also immensely expensive and depersonalizes the relationship between those in need of aid and those giving it.

Rocco Buttiglione elaborates on these views expressed in *Centesimus Annus.* Commenting on the structural inadequacy of the welfare state, Buttiglione observes that many needs that demand state intervention stem from the contemporary crisis of the family. Moreover, in undertaking social and educational care, the state has limited the activities of the Church in these domains. "The task of the state in the domain of education and social welfare," Buttiglione writes, "is not only and not primarily to satisfy needs, but rather to stimulate and to promote solidarity through investment of resources in families or other communities engaged in these areas and anticipating those needs which the market cannot satisfy."[36] The Church is one of those mediating institutions that allow society to flourish. Society suffers when the state hinders the Church's educational and charitable missions.

John Paul approvingly repeats the teachings of *Rerum Novarum* on limiting state intervention and on the primacy of the individual, family, and society. He recognizes that the state should intervene in certain circumstances, but such circumstances, he says, must involve "urgent reasons touching the common good." Even then, the pope declares, state intervention "must be as brief as possible." After all, when the state intervenes, it executes functions that other intermediary agencies could potentially perform. On the shoulders of these "various groups and associations" rests responsibility for the "exercise of human rights in the economic sector," John Paul writes. Excessive state intervention hinders "both economic and civil freedom."[37]

John Paul's vision of society makes clear that the state ought to limit its prerogatives and make itself available to serve the citizens. As Father Richard John Neuhaus put it, "The state . . . is not to be equated with the society. The state is one very important actor *within* society, and it is always to act as the servant, never as the master."[38] The pope's perspective implies the rejection not only of all theories that elevate the state to the absolute but also of the more moderate perspectives that support modern welfare states.[39]

None of this is to say that the pope endorses a laissez-faire perspective or looks to the state merely as a "night watchman." In fact, *Centesimus Annus* repeatedly critiques both of those perspectives. The institutions of state perform important functions, especially in realizing the common good.

Nevertheless, John Paul makes clear care that government interference should be kept to a minimum to ensure autonomy in all areas of social life. In the economic sector, the state should not take on invasive activity; its specific role consists in guaranteeing the rights and safety of working people. Above all, this means providing "sure guarantees of individual freedom and private property, as well as a stable currency and efficient public services," and "determining the juridical framework within which economic affairs are to be conducted, and thus of safeguarding the prerequisites of a free economy, which presumes a certain equality between the parties, such that one party would not be so powerful as practically to reduce the other to subservience."[40] Although *Centesimus Annus* suggests that ensuring that the rights of man are realized in the economic domain is another duty of the state, John Paul notes that the state should intervene only when the existence of a monopoly constitutes a danger to economic development.

For the pope, the state's task is to care for the good of all its citizens, which means, on the basis of the principle of solidarity, special care for the fate of the poorest and weakest: "a preferential option on behalf of the poor." From this option stems another responsibility: "society and the State will both assume responsibility" for protecting the worker from unemployment (by creating the conditions for full employment, providing social services, and facilitating training for new careers), for setting an honorable family wage and working hours, and for ensuring that workers are treated as persons rather than mere instruments of production.[41] Note the postulatory character of the pope's remarks, which point where the discussion should lead but do not insist on an ultimate solution. For example, in discussing society's and the state's shared responsibility for protecting people from unemployment, John Paul notes that "historically" workers have been protected "through economic policies aimed at ensuring balanced growth and full employment"; there is a crucial difference between that statement and a *demand* for full employment.

Note, too, John Paul's assertion that responsibility for the shape of economic life rests on "society and the State." Elsewhere the pope says that "*defending those collective goods* which, among others, constitute the essential framework for the legitimate pursuit of personal goals on the part of each individual" is a duty not only of the state but of "all of society." Taking the whole of the papal vision into account, one could easily conclude that society bears the primary responsibility; only when the social organization has failed to solve a problem is state intervention permitted.[42] When the pope does specify a "task of the state," he describes "the defence and preservation of common goods such as the natural and human environments, which cannot be safeguarded simply by market forces." Even here, John Paul does not call for interfering in market mechanisms; he simply underscores the fact that the free market cannot solve all social problems. When solutions lie beyond the boundaries of market action, and when the natural or human environment is endangered, the state *and society* should take appropriate measures.[43]

John Paul also raises the subject of the duties of states toward the international community. Already, in *Laborem Exercens*, the pope proposed that, whereas the fundamental issue of the nineteenth century was *"the 'class' question,"* the major challenge at the end of the twentieth was *"the 'world' question"*—that is, the search for solutions to social problems on a global level.[44] In *Centesimus Annus*, John Paul insists that cooperation and intervention on an international level are indispensable tools for the development of the most impoverished countries and for maintaining peace in the world.

In short, the state sketched in *Centesimus Annus* is not the welfare state, but neither is it an entity stripped of sensitivity and initiative. Its prerogatives are limited, but that does not mean it is weak. Harvard University's J. Bryan Hehir offers a good description: "The tension in John Paul's treatment of the state is that it both expresses his conviction that the state should be involved 'directly and indirectly' in fostering economic activity and in defending 'the weakest' participants in the economic sectors, and also reflects his determination to keep the power of the state limited by law and free of totalitarian pretensions."[45]

Thus the pope only outlines the framework within which the state functions. The border is constituted, on one hand, by the state's aspirations to totalitarianism (to some extent even the welfare state abuses its prerogatives) and, on the other hand, by political and economic mechanisms acting on their own accord. Between these two is a space that society should occupy. Broadly speaking, we could sum up these reflections simply: the less there is of the state, the better, because it is better to have "more society."

DEMOCRACY

What sort of state best embodies this social vision sketched in *Centesimus Annus*? Let us try to discern it by posing a slightly different question: What political system does the pope favor?

The answer is found in a passage where, indirectly, John Paul praises the "positive effort" some countries deployed after World War II to rebuild "a democratic society inspired by social justice." These efforts generally "preserve free market mechanisms, ensuring, by means of a stable currency and the harmony of social relations, the conditions for steady and healthy economic growth in which people through their own work can build a better future for themselves and their families." But he adds that the efforts also "try to avoid making market mechanisms the only point of reference for social life," meaning that society and the state work together to provide employment opportunities, professional formation, social security, freedom of association, and opportunities for democratic participation in the life of society. All of these elements, the pope says, "are meant to deliver work from the mere condition of 'a commodity,' and to guarantee its dignity."[46]

Moreover, the pope twice mentions democracy favorably in his historical summary of the 1980s. He notes that the fall of several dictatorships and their replacement by democratic systems gives hope for eradicating the injustices accumulated in these countries.

He then offers a more explicit affirmation of democracy: "The Church values the democratic system inasmuch as it ensures the participation of citizens in making political choices, guarantees to the governed the possibility both of electing and holding accountable those who govern them, and of replacing them through peaceful means when appropriate. Thus she cannot encourage the formation of narrow ruling groups which usurp the power of the State for individual interests or for ideological ends."[47] These words mark an advance in Catholic social teaching. George Weigel aptly describes the evolution of "the Church's encounter with democracy" as a "process of transition from *hostility* (Gregory XVI and Pius IX) to *toleration* (Leo XIII and Pius XI) to *admiration* (Pius XII and John XXIII) to *endorsement* (Vatican II and John Paul II), and now . . . to *internal critique*."[48]

For John Paul, the essential values are present in the democratic system. By allowing broad participation of citizens in political decisions, democracy conforms to the vision of society and of the state laid out in the encyclical. This broad participation is an expression of the personal dignity of every man. This is not to say that the pope has suddenly abandoned his pluralistic, antimodel stance. Recall his emphatic declaration that "the Church has no models to present"; the Church can fulfill its mission under various systems, he says.

Moreover, as Weigel suggests by mentioning "internal critique," John Paul does not offer unmitigated praise for democracy. The broad participation that democracy provides also has a negative dimension, in that a majority government can easily neglect the rights of citizens who are in the minority. That is why John Paul supports "checks and balances" and the separation of government powers. "Such an ordering," he writes, "reflects a realistic vision of man's social nature, which calls for legislation capable of protecting the freedom of all. To that end, it is preferable that each power be balanced by other powers and by other spheres of responsibility which keep it within proper bounds."[49]

In the same paragraph, the pope addresses "the principle of the 'rule of law,' in which the law is sovereign, and not the arbitrary will of individuals." He reaffirms this view when he writes, "Authentic democracy is possible only in a State ruled by law, and on the basis of a correct conception of the human person."[50] In endorsing the rule of law, John Paul supports one of the foundations on which Western democracies are built. This position is particularly significant given that he writes in the immediate aftermath of the collapse of communism, as the people of Central and Eastern Europe attempted to transform their own political systems.

Here again, although the pope endorses liberal democratic systems, he does not see them as a panacea, or as sufficient unto themselves. The rule of law only creates certain procedures and an institutional framework whose aim is to preserve the legal order. It cannot claim to resolve all the conflicts that arise in democratic societies. The very concept of the rule of law is built on a political philosophy that recognizes the essential role of values. As political scientist Bernhard Sutor remarked, "Some citizens, including Christians, tend to think that the institutions and regulations of a state ruled by law have a strictly formal character and the most important thing is to conduct a sound policy—something which is easiest for a strong government, which is not overly restricted and controlled."[51] But democracy involves more than the formal structures and rules; it depends on principles derived from a certain vision of man and his nature. As we will see in more detail in chapter 4, at the center of John Paul's anthropology is the view of the transcendent dignity of the person. Man's rights derive from that dignity.[52] The pope recognizes that in identifying a transcendent truth about man, he is challenging much of contemporary political thought.[53] John Paul writes: "Nowadays there is a tendency to claim that agnosticism and sceptical relativism are the philosophy and the basic attitude which correspond to democratic forms of political life. Those who are convinced that they know the truth and firmly adhere to it are considered unreliable from a democratic point of view." Nevertheless, the pope continues, "if there is no ultimate truth to guide and direct political activity, then ideas and convictions can easily be manipulated for reasons of power. As history demonstrates, a democracy without values easily turns into open or thinly disguised totalitarianism."[54] Elsewhere he declares, "Totalitarianism arises out of a denial of truth in the objective sense. If there is no transcendent truth . . . then the force of power takes over."[55]

These thoughts are crucial to John Paul's reflections on democracy. The pope himself highlighted the importance of these passages by citing them in two of his later encyclicals, *Veritatis Splendor* (1993) and *Evangelium Vitae* (1995).

These three encyclicals, whose extracts figure also in *The Catechism of the Catholic Church*, to a significant degree define his pontificate.

John Paul's thoughts reflect an evolution in the Church's teaching. Especially by interpreting the experience of totalitarianism, the Church has introduced a distinction between ideology and faith, openly opposing religious fundamentalisms and attempts to ideologize the state. Political scientists and advocates of the modern state, on the other hand, have nearly completely lost the certitude that absolute truth can be discovered by human reason (a certitude widespread at the outset, present in the works of Hugo Grotius, John Locke, Adam Smith, and many others).[56] That is to say, we have witnessed a shift from political agnosticism—not judging the authenticity of any particular conviction—toward an *ideological* agnosticism, rejecting the very idea of absolute truth.

As such, John Paul's comments on the concept of absolute truth are rather bold in an era of pluralism and cultural diversity.[57] But ideological agnosticism and its accompanying relativism endanger the very foundations of a democratic system.[58] After all, a liberal democratic state cannot be established in an axiological void, for it implies concrete ethical foundations. According to legal philosopher Ernst-Wolfgang Böckenförde, "Each statutory form of State understood as more than formal has its own ethos. The order it represents does not arise spontaneously from any anterior situation, but is ultimately the effect of a human action. . . . And because this is an order binding men, beings who are characteristically individual as well as communitarian, a certain ethos exterior to it is 'supplied' to serve as a foundation. Respect for this ethos makes the order of the State intrinsically possible, and, for this reason, it can be recognized as the skeleton of the common good."[59] This assertion is of capital importance for a liberal democracy, which cannot survive without some consensus concerning the "core of the common good"[60]—the system's foundations as well as the community's goals and the means it uses to realize them.[61]

To survive, a democratic system requires a certain anthropological minimum, a common vision of man shared by at least a clear majority of the actors in the democratic process. John Paul suggests that it is necessary to extend and deepen this consensus and to graft it on the transcendent truth of the dignity of man.

Five fundamental conditions (which form an integral part of a Christian anthropology) are surely elements of this anthropological minimum:

> (1) *Certitude that the actors in a democratic society are equal*: In democracies of antiquity (such as Athens), only about 12 to 15 percent of the population was involved in the democratic process. Today, in a world shaped by two thousand years of Christianity and marked by the American and the French Revolutions and a universal recognition of the rights of man, a democracy that forthrightly excludes some social group from its ranks is unthinkable. In the words of Bernhard Sutor, "After the fall of the old order, which was established on religious foundations, a society is no longer built on any other values except a human dignity common to all, and on the rights derived from

that belief."[62] That said, the belief that all members of a democratic society are equal is evident only in countries with Christian roots. It has not been accepted in the majority of cultures.

(2) Intellectual optimism: The democratic order is equally anchored in the conviction that man is apt to know reality, to face it in a reasonable manner, and to draw lessons from the experience acquired. In other words, this order is rooted in the conviction that the majority of the people will behave rationally. This conviction is not, however, evident in many other philosophical and religious currents. Nor is trust in rational and empirical knowledge common in other traditions.[63]

(3) Moral optimism: There can be no democracy without the presupposition that men are prepared to distinguish good from bad, and that at least the majority is apt to choose the good—not only out of a fear of punishment but also based on a conviction that it is right. In *The Moral Foundation of Democracy*, political philosopher John H. Hallowell wrote, "Preserving freedom demands reclaiming a belief both in the human capability of recognizing good, as in the ability to be guided by it within the limits imposed by historical circumstances and those resulting from the weaknesses of his will."[64]

(4) Realizing the common good as the raison d'être of the political community: It would be false to conclude

that there is some standard mold in which social life should be cast or a theoretical ideal to incarnate no matter the social cost.[65] Instead, there is a common denominator of an objective good to pursue, permitting a debate among citizens about how exactly their life together can be improved. The essence of democratic debate resides in the conviction that it is possible to find the most equitable manner of realizing the good of all citizens.

When this conviction is lacking—when it seems that evil exists only for me and for my own, or even that good exists only for me and for my own—politics becomes an art of gathering a majority from precarious alliances among minorities. As Hallowell pointed out, although democratic debate can never be totally rational, the pursuit of the common good elevates discussion above the mere competition of private interests.[66] F. A. Hayek noted that as democratic governments gain more power, they are "forced to bring together and keep together a majority by satisfying the demands of a multitude of special interests, each of which will consent to the special benefits granted to other groups only at the price of their own special interests being equally considered."[67]

(5) Generosity toward minority groups: The tyranny of the majority has long been seen as a potential threat to democracy. As Italian political scientist Giovanni Sartori put it, "If the majority criterion is turned (erroneously) into an absolute majority rule, the real-world implication of this switch is that a part

of the people (often a very large one) becomes a non-people, an excluded part."[68] This destabilizes the democratic order, as American political scientist Anthony Arblaster noted: "A democracy in which some groups, ethnic, religious, or political are permanently in a minority, and so in opposition, is likely to be unstable and may lose legitimacy."[69] That is why, wrote Hayek, "a society will achieve a coherent and self-consistent overall order only if it submits to general rules in its particular decisions, and does not permit even the majority to break these rules."[70]

History (the authority for the most enlightened thinkers) and our own prudence teach us that these\ five conditions are indispensable for the survival of a democratic state. Democracy is based on principles whose acceptance is, ultimately, an act of faith. As Jacques Maritain wrote, "A society of free men implies basic tenets which are at the core of its very existence. A genuine democracy implies a fundamental agreement between minds and wills on the bases of life in common; it is aware of itself and of its principles, and it must be capable of defending and promoting its own conception of social and political life; it must bear within itself a common human creed, the creed of freedom."[71]

Despite formulations such as "a fundamental agreement between minds and wills," this democracy is miles away from the ideological or confessional state. Maritain stressed that "this faith and inspiration, and the concept of itself which democracy needs—all these do not belong to the order of religious creed and eternal life, but to the temporal or secular order of earthly life, of culture or civilization." He added, "The faith in question is a civic or secular faith, that adherence forced upon all by reason's demonstrations, which the XVIIIth and XIXth Century philosophers sought in vain. A genuine democracy cannot impose on its citizens or demand from them, as a condition for their belonging to the city, any philosophic or any religious creed."[72]

Here we plunge into a sort of internal contradiction. Böckenförde captured the issue when he wrote, "The State can exist as a liberal State only because the freedom which it assures to citizens will be regulated from inside, by virtue of the moral substance of the individual and of the union of minds in society. On the other hand, the State cannot guarantee the existence of this moral substance by means of juridical constraint or an authoritarian injunction; it cannot do this without renouncing its liberalism."[73] This "Böckenförde paradox" recognizes that the foundation of liberal democracy is something that liberal democracy itself cannot guarantee. Or as Francis Fukuyama puts it, "Liberal democracies . . . are not self-sufficient: the community life on which they depend must ultimately come from a source different from liberalism itself."[74]

In *Centesimus Annus*, John Paul succinctly states his position: "In a world without truth, freedom loses its foundation."[75] In other words, freedom cannot be the sole objective of democracy; the objectives should be freedom *and* justice—that is to say, freedom and the construction of a common good.[76]

The triad *truth-morality-law* and the dyad *truth-freedom* are immutable and indispensable for the existence of democracy; by contrast, agnosticism and relativism erode the democratic ethos and produce atomization of society, which leads to anarchy or totalitarianism. John Paul's assertions here represent—in my opinion—the quintessence of his thought on contemporary democracy. Critics often claim that his discussions of truth, agnosticism, and "authentic democracy" express authoritarian aspirations of the papacy or of Catholicism. Such criticisms overlook the important point that, almost immediately after expressing his reservations about contemporary agnosticism and relativism, the pope adds that the Catholic faith is not an ideology and does not hold a magic recipe for administering life in society. This is where the pope states that "the Church's method is always that of respect for freedom." At the heart of the pontifical vision of social life is the affirmation that man is by his nature a being created for freedom.

John Paul underscores the importance of freedom in his warnings against collectivism. As much as he criticizes individualism and the ideology of the "minimum state," he rejects authoritarianism fundamentalism in the public forum. The pope points out, "In some countries new forms of religious fundamentalism are emerging which covertly, or even openly, deny to citizens of faiths other than that of the majority the full exercise of their civil and religious rights." This will not do, for, he declares, "the primary foundation of every authentically free political order" rests on recognition of "*the rights of the human conscience.*"[77]

Examined from an anthropological point of view, liberal democracy possesses the qualities essential to respecting the dignity of persons. More than any tutelary system, it offers citizens the possibility of participation in the political sphere. Furthermore, governments composed of democratically elected representatives are easier to control than are other regimes. Democracy also sets mechanisms in motion for a natural exchange of ruling elites. Finally, an absence of democracy, and consequently a lack of appropriate structures, leads to a system that tends to disregard the dignity of man and to limit his freedom, the spirit of enterprise, and solidarity.

All the same, the pope does not go so far as to conclude that democracy is the best, or even the closest to Christianity, of all existing political systems. His approval of democracy is rather reserved (though his praise is more explicit than that of his predecessors). He also draws attention to the inherent instability of democracy and the problems that result from depending on the will of the majority.

In reconstructing the position of *Centesimus Annus*, one can say that, from the Christian point of view, it is possible to affirm that a democratic system supplies the desirable anthropological minimum—that it corresponds to a realist vision of the human person. (The same cannot be claimed of any ideological and authoritarian state.)

FOUNDATIONS

Pope John Paul II's qualified praise for liberal democracy reflects the conviction that democratic systems provide the necessary minimum. But it is crucial to remember that society is not made up of a political system alone. John Paul outlines the important responsibilities of society's mediating institutions, especially the family, which stabilize and develop the social fabric. He also emphasizes that a society whose political philosophy is relativism is threatened by self-destruction. The pope stresses absolute and immutable foundations that recognize the essential rights and dignity of man.

John Paul thus describes life in society based on a transcendent truth, a truth that animates social life, including the sphere understood by the logic of the gift. Recognizing the great complexity of human reality, this vision permits a wide range of concrete, detailed solutions. John Paul renounces the project of describing social reality in a complete, hermetic way that would risk being ideologized. He also asserts that neither democracy nor capitalism can be protected from failure if these systems assume the automatic working of the market economy and of democratic mechanisms or accept an ideological agnosticism as the constitutive principle of the public forum.

The pope's warnings are neither a critique of democracy, as the advocates of other systemic solutions have portrayed them, nor some anachronistic reproach generated by a misunderstanding of the realities of the contemporary world, as certain democratic militants have complained. Exempt from all ideology, John Paul's project is founded on respect for human dignity, and thus for human freedom, whose political expression is the state ruled by law and endowed with a market economy. The pope's criticism of liberal democracy is made from within, but that does not prevent it from reaching democracy's very foundations.

THREE

ECONOMIC LIFE

Pope John Paul II's analysis of economic life in *Centesimus Annus* revolves around three themes. First, he offers a criticism of "unbridled capitalism," based on its historical symptoms. Next, he criticizes negative contemporary manifestations of the market economy, while highlighting the positive aspects of capitalism as it evolved in the course of the twentieth century. Finally, he sketches a vision of economic life as it would appear if Catholic social teaching were widely implemented.

A Critique of "Unbridled Capitalism"

The critique of "unbridled capitalism" calls attention to the complaints Leo XIII formulated in *Rerum Novarum*. John Paul twice emphasizes that Leo's critique should not be dismissed as applying only to the nineteenth century. Certain elements of his predecessor's missive have retained their currency.

John Paul addresses two reproaches to the liberal democracy just beginning to grow in the nineteenth century—namely, infringements on justice and injuries to human dignity: "A traditional society was passing away and another was beginning to be formed—one which brought the hope of new freedoms but also the threat of new forms of injustice and servitude."[1] These threats developed from political, economic, and social disorders; scientific and technical transformations; and the birth of ideologies that posited a new conception of society and of the state and a new structure of production, all based on a "strict individualism" or even "total economic freedom." John Paul sums up the situation at the end of the nineteenth century: "Pope Leo XIII and the Church with him were confronted, as was the civil community, by a society which was torn by a conflict all the more harsh and inhumane because it knew no rule or regulation."[2]

In effect, the rhythm of production became subject to the pursuit of profit alone, without regard to the family situation, sex, or age of employees. Labor became exclusively a commodity, whose price was established independent of the minimum standard of living. With unemployment a constant threat, workers faced the specter of famine. John Paul cites Leo's complaints against the state for "'favouring one portion of the citizens,' namely the rich and prosperous," instead of helping "the defenseless and the poor." The result, in Leo's words, was "a society divided into two classes, separated by a deep chasm."[3]

Leo's description of capitalism in *Rerum Novarum,*
which John Paul develops in *Centesimus Annus,* highlights how the ideologies professed by capitalism's master
thinkers, as well as the economic realities of the time, led
to the dehumanization of social life and aggravated social
inequalities.[4] Even authors favorable to liberal and capitalist institutions, such as the economist Wilhelm Röpke and
the American sociologist Peter Berger, acknowledge the
gravity of the problem.

In the nineteenth century, writes Röpke,

> Life becomes de-humanized and man becomes the
> plaything of unhuman, pitiless forces. . . . Hence the
> increasing indifference to all matters of collective
> ethics, hence scientific positivism and relativism. . . .
> It further leads to a fanatical belief in a mechanical
> causality even outside the processes of nature . . . to
> social laws such as Malthus' "law of population," or
> Lassalle's "immutable law of wages"; to the oriental-
> baroque flirtation with fate; in brief to determin-
> ism which not only is raised anew to a philosophic
> dogma, but also dominates sociology, be it in the
> garb of Marx's materialist view of history, be it in that
> of the geographic determinism, as first developed by
> Ritter and Ratzel . . . or be it finally as biological or
> even merely zoological determinism, the final degra-
> dation that could be reached along that path.[5]

This intellectual atmosphere bore some responsibility for the accumulation of social injustices. According to
Berger, "In all Western capitalist societies, the Industrial

Revolution was accompanied by a sharp and long-lasting increase in inequality. . . . By the late nineteenth century, there was very high inequality in all industrial or industrializing countries, highest of all in Britain (where, indeed, it was greater than in most Third World countries today)."[6]

The early stages of capitalism brought the decline of many traditional workshops as working hours were prolonged and the cheapest labor—child labor—was pitilessly exploited.[7] The state aggravated this injustice still more, often supporting capitalists at the expense of workers.

Rodger Charles, SJ, an authority on Catholic social doctrine, describes the hypocrisy of the system:

> In America a double standard was accepted. If businessmen combined to further their own purposes, this was in accordance with natural law, but if labour did the same, it was a conspiracy. Likewise, monopoly was good business, but the closed shop for trade unionists was un-American. The government had a responsibility to aid business and protect its interests, but if it did the same for labour then that was socialism. That business should influence politics was considered common-sense—but that labour should, was un-American. Those who owned property had a natural right to get a fair return on it—but all labour might demand was simply the going market price. Hence, appeals to protect or to develop property interests were reasonable, but if the same was invoked in labour's favour, then this was unreasonable. And what was true of economic and indus-

trial development in America and Britain was true of continental Europe too.[8]

The doctrine of the free economy, considering the political and economic advantages of its defenders, tipped the scales in favor of the stronger. Profit became a tool of injustice as the wealthy bought influence in the legal and political systems.

Having denounced "the strict individualism," "the *total* economic freedom," and "the pitiless social conflict" that characterized early capitalism, John Paul calls out the dehumanization of the world of work. This dehumanization was reflective of a mentality that the pope identifies elsewhere with the Enlightenment, a mentality that apprehended "human and social reality in a mechanistic way."[9] Increasingly, man was treated in an instrumental, even inhuman, way.

British economic historian R. H. Tawney notes that in the early years of capitalism, new ideas pushed aside "the conception that a moral rule is binding on Christians in their economic transactions." A "new science of Political Arithmetic" emerged, asserting "that no moral rule beyond the letter of the law exists." This new science was "influenced in its method by the contemporary progress of mathematics and physics" and thus treated "economic phenomena, not as a casuist, concerned to distinguish right from wrong, but as a scientist, applying a new calculus to impersonal economic forces."[10]

The target of Pope Leo's and Pope John Paul's critiques is not capitalism per se but rather *economism,* a mechanistic and materialistic concept of human activity. In fact, it would be misleading to present a balance sheet of the nineteenth century in which all the debts are charged to capitalism and none of the credits. For example, compare the situation of the proletariat with the conditions of equivalent classes in precapitalist societies. Capitalism developed in places where peasants were subjected to iniquitous treatments such as statute labor, where child labor was exploited, and where day labor was widespread in workshops, factories, and agriculture, labor that was paid according to a market minimum—that is, well below the essential minimum. These deplorable conditions were not capitalist innovations.[11] In *How the West Grew Rich*, Nathan Rosenberg and L. E. Birdzell Jr. write: "The romantic view that workers in pre-industrial Europe lived well may safely be dismissed as pure fantasy. If early factory work was oppressive, the alternatives open to those who voted with their feet for factory work were worse. The early factories were able to attract workers with low wages because the wages were still . . . better than anything available elsewhere to an impoverished agricultural population."[12]

Why, then, did capitalism bear so much criticism for conditions that predated capitalist systems? One explanation involves the development of a moral consciousness that recognized the dignity of each individual being. As cultural historian Christopher Dawson put it, "It is true that the worst results of modern industrialism cannot be compared with the horrors of the Roman slave system, but the existence of the modern ideals of humanity and liberty has caused the evils of the modern system to be far more strongly felt."[13]

One cannot ignore the achievements of capitalism:

dynamic increases in production, earnings,[14] and living conditions.[15] Economic historian T. S. Ashton writes, "During the period 1790–1830 factory production increased rapidly. A greater proportion of the people came to benefit from it both as producers and as consumers." Ashton cites declining prices, new and better products, the rise of new industries (and thus new jobs), and the growth of trade unions, banks, newspapers, schools, and other mediating institutions—all of which "give evidence of the existence of a large class raised well above the level of mere subsistence."[16]

CRITICISM OF CONTEMPORARY CAPITALISM

When John Paul refers to the "enormous wealth of the few as opposed to the poverty of the many,"[17] one should note that the extreme inequalities brought about by early capitalism did not persist. Nobel Prize–winning economist Simon Kuznets shows that in the period of modern economic growth, inequalities in income levels quickly rose at first but then clearly decreased, in effect eliminating egregious disproportions in wealth.[18] Indeed, in the century between *Rerum Novarum* and *Centesimus Annus,* the free-market economy underwent a significant and, generally speaking, positive evolution, bringing great growth in prosperity, limiting most abuses through legal frameworks, and providing a meaningful increase in social welfare, for the employed as well as the unemployed. Many of faults of the free-market economy that were widespread in the nineteenth century are less evident today.

This does not mean, however, that the Church sees no problems with contemporary capitalist systems. John Paul identifies one great deficiency plaguing our world economy: the inequity that leaves some people (predominantly those in developing nations) marginalized by the market or living under conditions "in which the struggle for a bare minimum is uppermost. These are situations in which the rules of the earliest period of capitalism still flourish in conditions of 'ruthlessness' in no way inferior to the darkest moments of the first phase of industrialization."[19]

Consistent with his critique of economism, the pope focuses more of his criticism on the error of believing that economic reality is the only reality—what he calls the "absolutizing" of economic life. He reminds us that "the economy in fact is only one aspect and one dimension of the whole of human activity." If the economy is absolutized, then "production and consumption of goods become the center of social life and society's only value." Such an absolutist approach expresses disdain for the dignity of the human person. John Paul warns against "the risk of an 'idolatry' of the market," because "there are collective and qualitative needs which cannot be satisfied by market mechanisms. There are important human needs which escape its logic. There are goods which by their very nature cannot be bought or sold." That is why he rejects a "system in which freedom in the economic sector is not circumscribed within a strong juridical framework which places it at the service of human freedom in its totality and sees it as a particular aspect of that freedom, the core of which is ethical and religious." Economic freedom must be framed within a just legal order because "economic freedom is only one element of human freedom"; when economic freedom is seen as the *only* freedom, it "loses its necessary relationship to the human person and ends up by alienating and oppressing him."[20]

The concern for human freedom and human dignity leads John Paul to caution against radical laissez-faire ideology, which avoids scrutinizing the problems of poverty, exploitation, and alienation, leaving their solution to the free play of market forces. The pope also warns against the ruthless domination of capital and the view that profit is the sole purpose of business and the decisive marker of industry's success.

Human labor and man himself, John Paul insists, must not be reduced to the level of ordinary merchandise, nor should a person be treated "more as a producer or consumer of goods than as a subject who produces and consumes in order to live." The pope explains how modern consumerist societies can reduce the person in this way: "In developed countries there is sometimes an excessive promotion of purely utilitarian values, with an appeal to the appetites and inclinations toward immediate gratification." A person can fall prey to such values through "manipulation by the means of mass communication, which impose fashions and trends of opinion through carefully orchestrated repetition."[21]

The pope, setting aside the question of whether such propaganda is a cause or a product of the consumer culture, emphasizes the broader cultural significance of this phenomenon. It manifests a specific concept of man: "The manner in which new needs arise and are defined is always marked by a more or less appropriate concept of man and of his true good. A given culture reveals its overall understanding of life through the choices it makes in production and consumption. It is here that *the phenomenon of consumerism* arises. In singling out new needs and new means to meet them, one must be guided by a comprehensive picture of man which respects all the dimensions of his being."[22]

An integral vision of man contains a social dimension. Therefore, the pope writes, "Development must not be understood solely in economic terms, but in a way that is fully human. It is not only a question of raising all peoples to the level currently enjoyed by the richest countries, but rather of building up a more decent life through united labor, of concretely enhancing every individual's dignity and creativity, as well as his capacity to respond to his personal vocation, and thus to God's call."[23]

Without this transcendental reference point—without "a comprehensive picture of man which respects all the dimensions of his being and which subordinates his material and instinctive dimensions to his interior and spiritual ones"—the human being is reduced to the material, the instinctive, and the sensory. As a result, people "are led to consider themselves and their lives as a series of sensations to be experienced" and aim to experience as much fun as possible in life.[24]

Such hedonism, taking root especially in immature and weak personalities, has destructive repercussions across the social landscape. The pope writes, "If a direct appeal is made to human instincts—while ignoring in various ways the reality of the person as intelligent and free—then *consumer attitudes* and *life-styles* can be created which are objectively improper and often damaging to the person's physical and spiritual health." He adds, "A striking example of artificial consumption contrary to the health and dignity of the human person, and certainly not easy to control, is the use of drugs." This and other manifestations of consumerism stem from a negation of the transcendent dimension: "Drugs, as well as pornography and other forms of consumerism which exploit the frailty of the weak, tend to fill the resulting spiritual void."[25]

Thus we arrive at the crux of the problem: the alienation of man. The pope explains: "A person who is concerned solely or primarily with possessing and enjoying, who is no longer able to control his instincts and passions, or to subordinate them by obedience to the truth, cannot be free: *obedience to the truth* about God and man is the first condition of freedom, making it possible for a person to order his needs and desires and to choose the means of satisfying them according to a correct scale of values, so that the ownership of things may become an occasion of personal growth." Consumerism that rejects or at least ignores the need for obedience to transcendental truths locks the person "within a selfishness which ultimately harms both him and others."[26]

The pope's argument about economic life thus parallels his description of political community seen in the previous chapter. In the economy as in the political sphere, ideology constitutes a threat to the person and to society. Absolutizing ownership, profit, and freedom of the market leads to the ideology of capitalism, which in turn makes the human being the object of the play of the free market. This capitalist ideology is really a form of utilitarian philosophy. In making idols of free-market institutions and absolutizing the economic dimension, it leads to consumerism, that contemporary version of hedonism, which rejects the transcendental dimension of the human being and leads to an inner imprisonment.

True, a tendency to concentrate primarily on the immoderate consumption or exploitation of goods can be observed among people living in various eras and cultures. But capitalist ideology spreads and strengthens such an attitude and even gives it moral sanction. In this context the pope refuses to grant consumer society superiority over Marxist solutions, since consumerism, too, alienates and depersonalizes the human individual. For instance, he writes that "insofar as [a consumer society] denies an autonomous existence and value to morality, law, culture and religion, it agrees with Marxism, in the sense that it totally reduces man to the sphere of economics and the satisfaction of material needs."[27]

From these observations, one is led to ask two questions. First, is this view of capitalism too pessimistic, inspired solely by a religious perception of reality? Second, is the free-market economy, as the pope postulates, inescapably connected with capitalist ideology?

To answer the first question, one should remember that even if those who propagate capitalist ideology are few in number, they are often influential opinion makers. Economist Milton Friedman, political philosopher Robert Nozick, and Objectivist philosopher Ayn Rand are among the most important representatives of this way of thinking.

Friedman, the distinguished monetarist from the University of Chicago, argues that there is no social responsibility in the economic sphere; in fact, he says, to call for such social responsibility is dangerous because that mindset leads to collectivism. Friedman writes, "There is one and only one social responsibility of business—to use it resources and engage in activities designed to increase its profits so long as it stays within the rules of the game, which is to say, engages in open and free competition without deception or fraud."[28] In the eyes of Ayn Rand, the free market is held in even higher esteem. It "represents the *social* application of an objective theory of values," allowing men "to think, to study, to translate their knowledge into physical form, to offer their products for trade, to judge them, and to choose, be it material goods or ideas, a loaf of bread or a philosophical treatise."[29] In the world she would have, men are judged as objects whose ideal is *homo economicus,* and the model society is a state ruled by money.[30] The only mediation permitted the state is defense against the violence of others.[31]

The libertarian approach to the right of private property, though theoretically not an absolute right, is in practice free of social and moral obligations. Consider this excerpt from Nozick:

> The fact that someone owns the total supply of something necessary for others to stay alive does *not* entail that his (or anyone's) appropriation of anything left some people (immediately or later) in a situation worse than the baseline one. A medical researcher who synthesizes a new substance that effectively treats a certain disease and who refuses to sell except on his terms does not worsen the situation of others

by depriving them of whatever he has appropriated. The others easily can possess the same materials he appropriated; the researcher's appropriation or purchase of chemicals didn't make those chemicals scarce in a way so as to violate the Lockean proviso [which holds that people can appropriate property from nature only as long as "there is enough, and as good, left in common for others"]. . . . The fact that the medical research uses easily available chemicals to synthesize the drug no more violates the Lockean proviso than does the fact that the only surgeon able to perform a particular operation eats easily obtainable food in order to stay alive and to have the energy to work.[32]

Such views of capitalism as a panacea for society's ills are extreme, but similar (albeit less radical) ideas are deeply rooted in today's culture. A common perspective associates any and all accomplishments of modernity with capitalism. The transition in Western culture from an urban society to a consumer society, which began in the early twentieth century and picked up speed after World War II, led to increasingly intense striving to satisfy desires.[33] In the 1980s consumerism became an even more obvious and essential element of culture. As one of the most famous postmodernist theorists, Jean Baudrillard, put it, "We are everywhere surrounded by the remarkable conspicuousness of consumption and affluence, established by the multiplication of objects, services, and material goods. This now constitutes a fundamental mutation in the ecology of the human species."[34]

One has to remember, however, that postmodernism is not merely a philosophical and elitist reflection but is becoming the dominant way of life for all of civilization. As political scientist Susan Meld Shell writes, "It is everywhere around us, winking at us from rock videos and commercials. . . . Today's nihilism is no *angst* and all play. *Spiel macht frei* [play will make you free]"[35]

From this brief review of the positions of economists, philosophers, and sociologists, it is fair to conclude that the answer to our first question is no—that is, John Paul's objections to contemporary liberal democracy are not inspired solely by religion, and there is ample evidence to indicate that his conclusions are not too pessimistic. Both phenomena the pope censures—capitalist ideology and consumerism—are indeed very much present in Western civilization today.

That brings us back to the second question: Are both phenomena the inevitable effects of a free-market economy? The answer to that question is also a definite no, as John Paul makes clear in the pages of his encyclical.

First of all, when he considers consumerism, John Paul clearly writes, "Of itself, an economic system does not possess criteria for correctly distinguishing new and higher forms of satisfying human needs from artificial new needs which hinder the formation of a mature personality."[36] Therefore, the free-market economy cannot alone be responsible for prevailing consumption. The pope's thesis can be interpreted either as an argument against a sort of "value blindness" on the part of the open market (which could be either good or bad) or as an assertion that the removal of ethics and culture from the economic sphere leads to idolatry of the market, which fosters an economic quasiculture characterized by a pragmatic-hedonistic value system. Lending credence to the first interpretation is the pope's suggestion that the cause of consumerism is the incorrect use of the institution of the free market (which in and of itself is a positive thing). In consumer culture "the innovative capacity of a free economy is brought to a one-sided and inadequate conclusion."[37] In either case, however, the crux of the problem lies in *culture*.

John Paul emphasizes the cultural dimension when he reaches into the roots of the problem, writing that the genesis of consumerism and the genesis of capitalist ideology are not located in the economic sphere. Culture generates and reinforces both these phenomena if its ethical and religious dimensions are weakened. Hence, after a series of critical comments on the situation in today's world, John Paul adds:

> These criticisms are directed not so much against an economic system as against an ethical and cultural system. The economy in fact is only one aspect and one dimension of the whole of human activity. If economic life is absolutized, if the production and consumption of goods become the center of social life and society's only value, not subject to any other value, the reason is to be found not so much in the economic system itself as in the fact that the entire sociocultural system, by ignoring the ethical and religious dimension, has been weakened, and ends by limiting itself to the production of goods and services alone.[38]

Finally, John Paul describes the free market and its institutions in a positive way, implying that he does not consider them to be intrinsically flawed. This last point merits an extended discussion of its own.

THE FREE, CREATIVE, AND SYMPATHETIC PERSON IN THE FREE MARKET

John Paul's emphasis on the positive aspects of the market economy is a crucial novelty in the social teachings of the Church. Before *Centesimus Annus,* papal encyclicals only peripherally considered those positive aspects. Instead they focused on capitalism's negative effects and symptoms, or they had merely defended its fundamental institutions against attempts to abolish private property and market competition.

Throughout *Centesimus Annus* the pope notes the evolution in capitalist societies over the past hundred years. The most notable development is the great rise in prosperity. Previously, much of the world's population had to concentrate almost exclusively on material concerns—that is, on meeting the basic conditions for survival. The proliferation of better goods and service thus significantly improved quality of life for many people.

John Paul also reflects on the ever greater role man plays as a creative subject in economic life: "Whereas at one time the decisive factor of production was *the land,* and later capital—understood as a total complex of the instruments of production—today the decisive factor is increasingly *man himself,* that is, his knowledge, especially his scientific knowledge, his capacity for interrelated and compact organization, as well as his ability to perceive the needs of others and to satisfy them." The pope clearly regards this evolution in economic life as significant and beneficial—so much so, in fact, that he suggests capitalism as a desirable economic system in post-Communist or Third World countries: "If by 'capitalism' is meant an economic system which recognizes the fundamental and positive role of business, the market, private property and the resulting responsibility for the means of production, as well as free human creativity in the economic sector, then the answer is certainly in the affirmative."[39]

In addition to highlighting the positive change that came as human work overtook natural resources and capital as the decisive force in economic life, the pope praises the increasing social interdependence of workers: "More than ever, work is *work with others* and *work for others*. . . . Work becomes ever more fruitful and productive to the extent that people become more knowledgeable of the productive potentialities of the earth and more profoundly cognizant of the needs of those for whom their work is done." He adds, "Important virtues are involved in this process, such as diligence, industriousness, prudence in undertaking reasonable risks, reliability and fidelity in interpersonal relationships, as well as courage in carrying out decisions which are difficult and painful but necessary, both for the overall working of a business and in meeting possible setbacks."[40]

Such an economic system—one in which human labor becomes increasingly important, which prefers cooperation among people, which encourages several principal virtues, and which concurrently makes use of the creative abilities of the person and tries to satisfy human needs—conforms to, or at least converges with, a Christian anthropology that accents rationality (hence creative capability) and independence (hence moral responsibility) and the social nature of the human being. Analyzing the sources of wealth of developed nations, the pope points to three determining factors. The first is ownership of knowledge, technique, and talent: "The wealth of the industrialized nations is based much more on this kind of ownership than on natural resources." The second source of wealth is, according to John Paul, "the ability to foresee both the needs of others and the combinations of productive factors most adapted to satisfying those needs." The third is the existence of many goods that "cannot be adequately produced through the work of an isolated individual; they require the cooperation of many people in working toward a common goal. Organizing such a productive effort, planning its duration in time, making sure that it corresponds in a positive way to the demands which it must satisfy, and taking the necessary risks—all this too is a source of wealth in today's society." The pope concludes, "In this way, the *role* of disciplined and creative *human work* and, as an essential part of that work, *initiative and entrepreneurial ability* becomes increasingly evident and decisive."[41]

Only after these deliberations, conducted at the level of social philosophy, can a theological conclusion be reached: "This process [of entrepreneurial economic activity], which throws practical light on a truth about the person which Christianity has constantly affirmed, should be viewed carefully and favorably."[42]

Therefore, the true measure of an economic system, for John Paul, lies in whether it respects the truth about man as a person. This emphasis reflects what one commentator calls the "methodological anthropocentrism" of the pope's analysis.[43]

Stating explicitly that the Church "recognizes the positive value of the market and of enterprise," the pope applauds the fact that the basis of the modern *business economy* "is human freedom." He observes that free-market institutions "help to utilize resources better; they promote the exchange of products; above all they give central place to the person's desires and preferences, which, in a contract, meet the desires and preferences of another person." One way in which Marxism errs, he adds, is in "denying the legitimacy and positive value of market relationships even in their own sphere." Elsewhere, John Paul reminds us that "a business cannot be considered only as a 'society of capital goods'; it is also a 'society of persons' "—indeed, that its purpose is found in "its very existence as a *community of persons*."[44]

The encyclical includes still more affirmations of free-market principles and institutions. For example, John Paul writes that the Church recognizes the positive role of profit (as long as it is not the only regulator of a business) "as an indication that a business is functioning well." He explains, "When a firm makes a profit, this means that productive factors have been properly employed and corresponding human needs have been duly satisfied." Trying to suppress the profit motive limits not only the effective functioning of an enterprise but also human freedom and creativity: "Where self-interest is violently suppressed, it is replaced by a burdensome system of bureaucratic control which dries up the wellsprings of initiative and creativity."[45]

The pope examines one of the fundamental aspects of free markets: private property. The Church, he writes, has always defended "the necessity and therefore the legitimacy of private ownership." The right to private property "is fundamental for the autonomy and development of the person." Twice in *Centesimus Annus* the pope examines the roots of private ownership. First he writes, "It is through work that man, using his intelligence and exercising his freedom, succeeds in dominating the earth and making it a fitting home. In this way, he makes part of the earth his own, precisely the part which he has acquired through work; this is *the origin of individual private property*." Later he states the matter even more strongly: "Man fulfills himself by using his intelligence and freedom. In so doing he utilizes the things of this world as objects and instruments and makes them his own. The foundation of the right to private initiative and ownership is to be found in this activity." Because work plays such a key role—because a person "realizes himself" through it—"ownership of the means of production, whether in industry or agriculture, is just and legitimate if it serves useful work."[46]

But John Paul stresses that property ownership is not an absolute right: "It becomes illegitimate, however, when it is not utilized or when it serves to impede the work of others, in an effort to gain a profit which is not the result of the overall expansion of work and the wealth of society, but rather is the result of curbing them or of illicit exploitation, speculation or the breaking of solidarity among working people." Possession is inherently social in nature. The universal destination of material goods, a principle at the heart of Catholic social teaching, places social obligations on the owners of property.[47]

Here a convergence is clearly seen with the views John Paul expressed earlier in *Laborem Exercens,* where he wrote of "the person who becomes a person partly through his work," of ownership "through work," and the amorality of possession "despite work" or "in opposition to work." The key difference between these two encyclicals is that *Centesimus Annus* emphasizes more forcefully the advantages of private ownership.

One could draw a broader conclusion: that the pope has transferred to the pages of *Centesimus Annus* the anthropology of a free, creative, and solidaristic subject—or agent— of work outlined in *Laborem Exercens.* This time, however, John Paul situates the subject of *Laborum Exercens* in a democratic milieu and in the world of free-market institutions. As a result, the papal deliberations become more concrete, and John Pope can reformulate the expectations for the institutions of democratic capitalism. At the same time, he can illustrate the positive aspects of these institutions and how the principles on which they are founded converge with a Christian anthropology.

Given the novelty of John Paul's approach, one should ask whether the image of democratic capitalism offered here is too positive, too idealistic. Does such a vision of economics conform with real life?

Centesimus Annus indirectly provides an answer. When the pope discusses the phenomenon of "the spread of Communist totalitarianism over more than half of Europe and over other parts of the world," he outlines three ways of reacting to the Marxist challenge:

> (1) by building "a democratic society inspired by social justice, so as to deprive Communism of the revolutionary potential represented by masses of people subjected to exploitation and oppression";
> (2) by forming "systems of 'national security,' aimed at controlling the whole of society in a systematic way, in order to make Marxist infiltration impossible"; and
> (3) by developing "the consumer society," which "seeks to defeat Marxism on the level of pure materialism by showing how a free market society can achieve a greater satisfaction of material human needs than Communism."[48]

The second and third solutions, in the pope's view, are wrongheaded. The doctrine of "national security" limits the freedom of a society and permits the violation of human rights. In turn, a consumerist society reduces a person to the level of *homo economicus* and creates a hedonistic culture. This and the pope's other reflections on the dangers of consumerism show, in particular, an awareness of the dangers associated with free markets if they are not supported by an integral vision of human development. The attention devoted to these dangers clearly demonstrates that the encyclical's vision is not removed from reality.

John Paul's response to the first of these proposed solutions also indicates that his approach is not overly idealistic.

He expresses approval of efforts to build "a democratic society ruled by social justice":

> In general, such attempts endeavor to preserve free market mechanisms, ensuring, by means of a stable currency and the harmony of social relations, the conditions for steady and healthy economic growth in which people through their own work can build a better future for themselves and their families. At the same time, these attempts try to avoid making market mechanisms the only point of reference for social life, and they tend to subject them to public control which upholds the principle of the common destination of material goods. In this context, an abundance of work opportunities, a solid system of social security and professional training, the freedom to join trade unions and the effective action of unions, the assistance provided in cases of unemployment, the opportunities for democratic participation in the life of society—all these are meant to deliver work from the mere condition of "a commodity," and to guarantee its dignity.[49]

This broadly detailed description is not merely theoretical. It refers, to a certain extent, to all the Western democracies, but it applies to a greater degree to the socioeconomic reforms enacted in West Germany after World War II. The driving force behind these reforms were the Ordoliberals, a group of thinkers and political actors who sparked the German postwar "economic miracle" by setting up a social market economy.[50] The Ordoliberal vision may reasonably be seen as a precursor to the views expounded in *Centesimus Annus*.

THE PRECURSORS OF CENTESIMUS ANNUS

After the Second World War, Germany was a ruined nation. As one witness of the postwar period aptly noted, almost no one in 1945 could have predicted that the German economy would not only recover but would in two decades' time become one of the world's strongest. The remarkable rebuilding effort resulted from the creative cooperation of a broad group of thinkers—distinguished economic theorists (chief among them Walter Eucken), lawyers (such as Franz Böhm), economists who were also historians and philosophers (especially Wilhelm Röpke, the main author of the Ordoliberal theoretical program, as well as Alexander Rüstow), and economists who turned out to be illustrious politicians (including Minister of Economics—and later Chancellor—Ludwig Erhard and his adviser Alfred Müller-Armack). The breadth of knowledge and experience produced an accurate, multidimensional analysis of the causes of the capitalist crisis and a successful model for rebuilding economic life—one founded on a Christian anthropology and metaphysics. Contemporary German economist Theo Weigel wrote on the hundredth anniversary of Erhard's birth, "The social market economy is thus, ultimately, a successful synthesis between liberal concepts ruling politics and the social principles of Catholic social teaching."

Based on these principles, the Ordoliberal criticism of

capitalism acquired a spiritual dimension and was, in its depth, much more original—and, as it turned out, more effective—than John Maynard Keynes's prescription, which reacted more to the consequences of crises than to their causes. According to the Ordoliberals, Keynes's theories led Europe into sustained inflation and economic and social chaos after World War II,.

Ordoliberal thinkers operated on the basic principle that the spiritual dimension of human life cannot be ignored and therefore neither can the transcendent dignity of each person. In their view, the key failure of nineteenth-century liberalism lay in overlooking these vital elements. In *A Humane Economy*, Röpke writes: "The ultimate source of our civilization's disease is the spiritual and religious crisis which has overtaken all of us and which each must master for himself. Above all, man is *Homo religiosus*, and yet we have, for the past century, made the desperate attempt to get along without God, and in the place of God we have set up the cult of man, his profane or even ungodly science and art, his technical achievements, and his State."[51] According to the Ordoliberal critique, the Enlightenment influence on nineteenth-century culture included too much Rousseau and Voltaire and not enough Montesquieu.

This debate with Enlightenment thinking is reflected in the very name of the Ordoliberals. For Enlightenment thinkers, the ideal was *l'ordre naturel*—a spontaneous order in which rational and enlightened individuals acted in all areas of life. For the Ordoliberals, by contrast, the ideal was the *ordo universi*—the order of the universe, the idea that there was a natural order designed by God and directed by men. They had taken the idea from Thomas Aquinas, to whom they often referred. According to Franz Böhm, one of Walter Eucken's closest collaborators, there is only one system that deserves to be called an "order" in a higher sense: the created order of the universe. That is why the human goal should be to try as much as possible to grant priority, among all the systems, to that which has the nature of the *Ordo*. In the Ordoliberal view, it is precisely the lack of reference to the transcendent in contemporary liberalism that gave rise to the idolatry of economic life. Röpke wrote that economism "judges everything in relation to the economy and in terms of material productivity, making material and economic interests the center of things by deducing everything from them and subordinating everything to them as mere means to an end."[52] Economism led to three fundamental errors of liberalism: (1) an underappreciation of the importance of the ethical, legal, and institutional cornerstones of social life; (2) the failure to take human nature into account; and (3) the lack of critical reflection and the ability to make corrections.

Challenging economism, Ordoliberals identified the limitations of the free market. As if anticipating the words of *Centesimus Annus*, Röpke, while in exile during World War II, wrote: "Man's nature, therefore, sets definite limits to the rule of the market principle and in the same way as democracy must permit spheres free from the interference of the state, if it is not to degenerate into the worst kind of despotism, the market system, too must allow spheres free from the influence of the market, if it is not to become intolerable: there must be the sphere of community life and altruistic devotion, the sphere of self-sufficiency, the sphere of small and simple living conditions, the sphere of the state and of planned economy."[53] Modern thinkers failed to recognize these limits. As a result, they did not realize that "the competitive principle is by no means applicable in all fields of production without leading to grave difficulties," that "there are certain markets which function only more or less imperfectly," and that "we meet abuses of competition everywhere which must be regulated by the state."[54]

Röpke summed up the matter in *The Moral Foundations of Civil Society*, writing, "Market economy requires a firm framework which to be brief we will call anthropo-sociological." He concluded, "In other words, market economy is not everything."[55]

To acknowledge the limits of the free market was not to endorse central planning, however. Ordoliberals opposed statist approaches. Beginning in 1947, they laid out the vision for what Alfred Müller-Armack described as *freie oder soziale Marktwirtschaft*—a free and social market economy.[56] The Ordoliberal vision quickly become known by an abbreviated version of that phrase—as *social* market economy—but it is important to note the first word, *free*. Indeed, according to the Ordoliberals, only a free market can be truly social, able to recognize the real needs of society and then responding to them effectively. The market must also be part of higher-level structures, taking into account individual human nature and various dimensions of social life.

As a constitutive element of the social market economy, the "social state" assumes a specific anthropology. Here man is a free and creative subject, capable of accepting responsibility for himself and his own. The order of a social welfare state is based on certain basic values that are built into the entire system and that must be universally endorsed for the whole to function correctly. The social state is a synthesis of freedom and social justice, of personal responsibility and solidarity. To these basic values, on which the state is built, Theo Weigel adds the principles of personalism, solidarity, and subsidiarity, which overcome the tension between freedom and equality.

During World War II, Röpke sketched out just such a synthesis. It was based on four fundamental principles:

(1) A truly competitive market economy—that is, an economy that eliminates any and all forms of monopoly.

(2) An active political economy that creates the legal and moral framework of a democratic state, which ensures adherence to the rules of the economic game and whose interventions support market mechanisms. Röpke stresses that to avoid the dangers of collectivism, state interventions must be compatible with the market economy—for example, they cannot destroy the dynamic pricing mechanisms that accurately relay information throughout the market.

(3) A policy that strengthens economic and social structures and supports decentralization. A humane economy is based on widespread property ownership and distribution of income, is balanced (for example, between industry and agriculture), and supports small and medium-sized companies, not just massive firms.

(4) A policy that allows the market economy to prosper by dealing with *nonmarket* social problems.

For instance, Röpke argued for a social welfare system, investments in research and education, the humanization of work relationships, environmental protection, and especially government information policies that allow people throughout society to understand the political, economic, and cultural problems that confront the society, as well as the interdependencies between them.[57]

Leading figures of the Freiburg School, such as Walter Eucken and Franz Böhm, translated Röpke's holistic program into the language of economic principles. They called it the "mutual competition system" or "organized competition system." Seven elements constituted the core of this system:

(1) A price system that duly records the play of supply and demand;

(2) Money with stable buying power (a concern that informs suggestions for the shape of the banking system);

(3) Free access to the market, including international markets (a principle that leads to recommendations about freedom of employment, the customs system, patent law, and more);

(4) Protection and expansion of private ownership of the means of production;

(5) Freedom to make contracts and choose contract partners (albeit within the framework of the "mutual competition system" so as to counteract collusion or cartels in the marketplace);

(6) Material responsibility—that is to say, he who plans and decides is held responsible for the results, both negative and positive, of his actions;

(7) Stable economic policy, which means policy removed from current politics, to promote more rational decisions and innovations to minimize the unavoidable element of risk.

Reflecting Ordoliberal distrust of automatic market solutions,[58] Eucken and his colleagues added some "regulating principles":

(1) Intervention to prevent monopolies (for example, anticartel laws and agencies to ensure compliance with the rules of competition);

(2) Stabilization of the market (via monetary policies especially);

(3) Instruments of social correction, such as fiscal policies (mildly progressive taxes, social subventions, unemployment and welfare benefits) to counter market-led preferences for production of luxury goods at the expense of goods needed by the impoverished; tax policy to encourage widespread property ownership and stabilize the "social state"; mechanisms for dealing with social problems that generally fall outside the view of profit-driven participants in a market economy—for example, environmental protection and protection of work relations and conditions; opposition to correcting anomalies in the supply of available workers by forcing certain members of some members of society to enter the labor force (Ordoliberals

especially opposed forcing women into the workforce); (e) a "quality of life" policy, supported by the financing of public schools, health care, and the transportation, tourism, and recreational infrastructure.

These theoretical precepts did not meet with much acceptance in postwar Germany. As German political scientist Dieter Grosser commented, this project must have seemed utopian to a German population immersed in poverty. But in 1949, Germany's impoverishment was not simply material; its social fabric had been torn apart by the experiences of totalitarianism, the Holocaust, and war. Gustav Stolper, an Austrian economist and journalist who had been a politician in the Weimar Republic, revisited Germany in the aftermath of World War II. His book about the postwar reality of Germany painted a bleak picture. In it he wrote, "The German nation is ruined. It is fatally weakened in its biological substance, in its cultural and technical environment, in its moral fibre."[59]

At the time, most observers expected that the economic system would be repaired through nationalization and central planning. Such assumptions were justified by the great popularity (especially among laborers) of the Social Democratic Party (SPD), which was demanding the introduction of a socialist economy, and by the tenor of the Christian Democratic Union (CDU) convention in 1947, which called for the socialization of the coal and foundry industries and some elements of central planning. But Konrad Adenauer appreciated the Ordoliberals' values and chose Ludwig Erhard as his closest adviser. With Adenauer quickly rising in stature and consistently pushing Ordoliberal policies, *freie oder soziale Marktwirtschaft* became the CDU program after the 1949 convention.

A critical moment came when Erhard implemented— without the agreement of the occupying forces—a secretly prepared, radical monetary reform. The economic council of the CDU (*Wirtschaftsrat*) passed the reform by a vote of 50–37 after just over ten hours of discussion on Friday evening, June 18, 1948—and the measure was already in force on Sunday, June 20.[60] This first move was part of a larger reform of capital that favored private businessmen through varied rates of exchange between the reichsmark and the newly introduced deutsche mark and that eliminated speculative capital and the remaining Third Reich debt.

The first consequences of this liberalization of the economy were an increased cost of living and a sudden leap in unemployment. In response, labor unions called a general strike in November 1948.

But positive effects of the reform quickly became evident. In 1949, Germany's production level reached that of 1936. From 1950 until 1955, the per capita gross national product (GNP) doubled; unemployment decreased from 10.4 to 5.2 percent; and the trade deficit turned into a growing surplus. GNP continued to rise at around 8 percent annually throughout the 1950s, and real wages rose 75 percent during that decade.

In accord with the Ordoliberal program, housing construction (especially private homes and apartments) rose with lightning speed. Of particular note is the fact that among private investors, the working class (33 percent) outnumbered white-collar employees and executives (22 percent). Social services were also introduced one after another: in 1950 a system insuring war victims was established and pensions raised; in 1952 a fourteen-week paid maternity leave was introduced; in 1954 benefits for large families appeared; and in 1957 the pension reform included an annual cost-of-living increase.

Certainly one cannot attribute all the achievements of the German "economic miracle" to the Ordoliberals. Still, they deserve the lion's share of credit for ushering in so radical and so effective an economic and social reform.

Nevertheless, the Ordoliberal reform did not endure. It underwent a grave crisis in 1967 when then–finance minister Karl Schiller forced through a bill supporting stability and economic growth based on Keynesian elements. The definitive break with the postwar program came in 1969, when Ludwig Erhard's term as chancellor ended and SPD rule began with the election of Willy Brandt. There followed a far-reaching expansion of social benefits and bureaucratic apparatuses while the country began to succumb to the specific pressures of various interest groups. As Keynesianism became dominant, Germany—and other Western countries—evolved away from the "social state" and toward a "welfare state." The economy became politicized and the number and scope of government interventions increased, which led to fiscal crises and finally the nationalization and bureaucratization of social programs.

Closely connected with this institutional failure was a moral-cultural crisis that Polish political scientist Aniela Dylus tersely described as the development of a "postmodern mentality of demand" and the spread of an "ideology of subjective social rights." This grave, multidimensional structural crisis underscores the pertinence of the principles on which the Ordoliberals based their reform of the economy and state.[61]

Hence the political and economic community was weakened, becoming the site of a competition with no limits, an arena for the stronger to dominate the weaker. This development led to calls for statist solutions—solutions that "socialized" the person. Both the Ordoliberals and Pope John Paul pointed out (though using different words) that the socialist fallacy stems from this human socialization. In John Paul's words, "The fundamental error of socialism is anthropological in nature." Socialism reduces man "to a series of social relationships," and as a result "the concept of the person as the autonomous subject of moral decision disappears." The unavoidable consequence of this erroneous anthropology is a political system that violates the rights of the human person and an economic sphere that violates labor rights. The inevitable "inefficiency of the economic system," the pope adds, is "a consequence of the violation of the human rights to private initiative, to ownership of property and to freedom in the economic sector."

Thus, out of a humanitarian motivation arises an inhumane system. Recalling Leo XIII's diagnosis, John Paul emphasizes that socialism is a cure worse than the illness itself.[62]

EXPOSING THE FALSE CHOICE

Through his analysis of economic life, Pope John Paul II unmasks the false choice that has been presented so often through the decades (even within the Church): socialism or capitalism? To accept the positive elements contained in socialist ideals, as Pius XI correctly observed, one does not have to be a socialist at all. But socialism, understood as a system of exchange and production whose primary organizer and major owner is the state, leads to economic ruin and political violence.

By rejecting the false choice, John Paul can concentrate on a more important question: What sort of person acts in the sphere of a free economy? The moral-cultural system is so important because it addresses this question—because it gets to the purpose and meaning of the human person, human society, and human activity. A Christian vision of the human being and the world suggests other, closely connected questions: What political and economic institutions expand the sphere of human freedom, help a person engage in creative activity and nurture interpersonal ties, and direct special attention toward the weak and defenseless?

The pope's reply to these questions overlaps with the views of the Ordoliberals. The system that meets the demands of Catholic social teaching (which is not to say that it is the sole acceptable possibility) is a democratic state of law and a socially sensitive, free economy. Such a system, thanks especially to the principle of subsidiarity, strengthens civil society.

The foundation for such an order is the family. John Paul writes, "The first and fundamental structure for 'human ecology' is the family, in which man receives his first formative ideas about truth and goodness, and learns what it means to love and to be loved."[63] Similarly, Röpke called the family "the simplest and most genuine of communities," the institution that is "the original and imperishable basis of every higher community."[64]

Ordoliberalism also lines up with the papal vision in *Centesimus Annus* in that it rejected any and all forms of ideology—capitalist, liberal, or socialist—and attempted to create a social order built on an anthropology respecting the transcendent dignity of each person and arising out of his rationality and freedom. Starting from a Christian inspiration and from general anthropological and metaphysical postulates, Ordoliberals constructed a concrete political-economic program and brought it into practice.

A list of such key points of consensus between *Centesimus Annus* and the writings of the Ordoliberals would be nearly endless. Such overlap should not, however, be interpreted to mean that John Paul unequivocally supports the solutions of the German Ordoliberal school. Recall the pope's statement that Catholic social teaching permits numerous and varied solutions; its task is not to construct specific projects.

The great achievement of *Centesimus Annus* is to build a bridge between Catholic social teaching and contemporary political and economic thought. If Polish economist Janusz Lewandowski was correct when he said, in the late 1980s, that twentieth-century liberal thinkers generally did not understand the social teaching of the Catholic Church, then the publication of *Centesimus Annus* changed this situation in an important way.[65] The pope's anthropological approach, with his vision of the person as an independent, creative subject who realizes his humanity through work and working with others (already traced in *Laborem Exercens*), is now applied to the assessment and description of the institutions of democratic capitalism.

John Paul returns to the vision of social life sketched in *Rerum Novarum* and *Quadragesimo Anno* but endows it with a new dimension by stressing the categories of creativity and enterprise in his examination of contemporary economic reality. The pope's "methodological anthropocentrism" also permits him to identify Christian sources for many of the same liberal institutions that have in recent centuries often placed themselves in opposition to the Church and Christianity. In fact, these institutions could not have been embodied in Western culture without Christianity's reinterpretation of the Judaic and Greek traditions, which has given them an original mark. They would not have arisen without broad social acceptance of the anthropology Christianity brought to the history of mankind. That anthropology contained a crucial concept of the person, implying the dignity and equality of human beings, who are endowed with a social nature (to which both individualism and collectivism are an affront), at the heart of which are inscribed universalism (to recognize humanity's common nature and destiny), cognitive optimism (to push the boundaries of human knowledge), and a capacity to expand the limits of human freedom. It should be added that Christianity instituted the separation of political and spiritual power—even if this has not always been observed in history.

Illustrating the key (though, naturally, limited) consensus between Christian anthropology and that implied by free-market institutions, the encyclical shows the positive values that can be realized in democratic capitalism. But this perspective also enables a nonideological criticism of these institutions that stresses the primacy of culture over economics and politics. Thus, much more precisely and deeply than ever before, it is possible to show the dangers and opportunities that culture carries with it. As *National Review* editor in chief John O'Sullivan put it after the encyclical's release, "What is startling and important about *Centesimus Annus . . .* is that it is the first Vatican document to address realistically and subtly the state of affairs in which liberalism is both triumphant over socialism and at war with itself. That is why it is of interest far beyond the ranks of the Catholic faithful."[66]

The emphasis on culture brings the point of view expressed in *Centesimus Annus* closer to the position presented by so-called neoconservatives in the United States beginning in the 1970s.[67] It also renews discussion of the thought of classical liberals such as F. A. Hayek, Ludwig von Mises, Joseph Schumpeter, and Milton Friedman. Given that representatives of twentieth-century liberalism overlooked many of the vital considerations these thinkers raised, Pope John Paul II's contributions become all the more meaningful. We live in an age that demands answers to deep and pressing questions. *Centesimus Annus* points in the direction from which answers should come.

We also live in an age in which media, political debate, and popular commentary privilege economic indicators. But it is possible to see more and more clearly how central is the truth that politics and economics are connected with the whole of culture.[68] It is also becoming more and more evident that the widespread idea of total economic and political autonomy, joined to a general vision of the "open society," involves internal contradictions—contradictions that threaten the very existence of societies by undermining a moral-cultural consensus.

FOUR

THE PRIMACY OF CULTURE

Pope John Paul II accords special importance to the cultural sphere, arguing that it enjoys primacy over political and economic reality. In this chapter, we explore John Paul's understanding of the term *culture* and the anthropology he expounds in *Centesimus Annus*. In addition, we examine the reciprocal bonds between Catholic social teaching and anthropology, on the one hand, and the economic, political, and cultural spheres of social life on the other.

THE MEANING OF THE TERM *CULTURE*

"All human activity takes place within a culture and interacts with culture," the pope writes in *Centesimus Annus*, "For an adequate formation of a culture, the involvement of the whole man is required, whereby he exercises his creativity, intelligence, and knowledge of the world and of people. Furthermore, he displays his capacity for self-control, personal sacrifice, solidarity and readiness to promote the common good."[1]

As is evident from this statement, John Paul understands culture in a very broad sense, recognizing its fundamental meaning in the life of a person and of a society. It is precisely through culture that we can understand man and the communities he forms. From the analysis of the causes of *consumerism* described in the previous chapter, one could infer that economic realities (and all the more so those that come from the political sphere) are to a great extent only epiphenomena within the moral-cultural system. Other statements from the encyclical support this thesis: for example, "A given culture reveals its overall understanding of life through the choices it makes in production and consumption"; and "Even the decision to invest in one place rather than another, in one productive sector rather than another, is always *a moral and cultural choice*."[2]

Thus, although the subject of culture is not discussed systematically in *Centesimus Annus,* it is of decisive importance. Instead of delving into terminological problems and striving to create a clear definition of this concept,[3] the pope describes the key elements of culture and the conditions for its correct functioning. From the remarks scattered through the encyclical, however, it is possible to extract the definition of culture implicit in John Paul's approach.

To begin with, compare the pope's comments on culture with the definition given at Vatican II. The Fathers of the Second Vatican Council wrote in *Gaudium et Spes*, "The word 'culture' in the general sense refers to all those things which go to the refining and developing of man's diverse mental and physical endowments. He strives to subdue the earth by his knowledge and his labor; he humanizes social life both in the family and in the whole civic community through the improvement of customs and institutions; he expresses through his works the great spiritual experiences and aspirations of men throughout the ages; he communicates and preserves them to be an inspiration for the progress of many, even of all mankind."[4] They also asserted that culture means "the cultivation of the goods and values of nature."[5]

In *Centesimus Annus*, John Paul differs from this account of culture on three points:

(1) He perceives culture in a wider sense. According to Vatican II's description, culture is associated with progress, development, and perfection—spiritual as well as physical. For John Paul, however, culture has an ambivalent nature. In the preceding chapter, for instance, we saw that, for the pope, consumerism is primarily a cultural phenomenon. In writing about the current degradation of family life, John Paul uses the phrase the "culture of death."[6] The cultural sphere may therefore involve a negative dimension.

(2) If, according to the definition in *Gaudium et Spes*, culture possesses a transcendental dimension, it is a *horizontal* transcendence—that is, the transcendence of man over the world's natural order, the material order. But in John Paul's description of culture,

one can also find a *vertical* transcendence—man's connection with God—for "at the heart of every culture
lies the attitude man takes to the greatest mystery: the
mystery of God." From God, too, man acquires "the
capacity to transcend every social order."[7]

(3) Two types of community are stressed in the
Second Vatican Council's definition: the family and
the state. John Paul recognizes the family as having a
substantially greater role, and he also introduces the
category of "intermediary groups."[8] He speaks of the
state only at the very end.

One may therefore say that for John Paul, the cultural
space constitutes a sort of metalevel that embraces all the
moral and theological problems, as well as political and
economic questions. Such an understanding of culture
is compatible with the description offered by the distinguished American philosopher Allan Bloom: "[Culture]
joins nature as a standard for the judgment of men and
their deeds but has even greater dignity. It is almost never
used pejoratively, as are 'society,' 'state,' 'nation' or even
'civilization,' terms for which culture is gradually substi-
tuted, or whose legitimacy is underwritten by culture. Culture is the unity of man's brutish nature and all the arts
and sciences he acquired in his movement from the state of
nature to civil society. Culture restores the lost wholeness
of first man on a higher level, where his faculties can be
fully developed without contradiction between the desires
of nature and the moral imperatives of his social life."[9]

Similarly, theologian and ethicist H. Richard Niebuhr
observed: "Man not only speaks but thinks with the aid of

the language of culture. Not only has the objective world about him been modified by human achievement; but the forms and attitudes of his mind which allow him to make sense out of the objective world have been given him by culture. He cannot dismiss the philosophy and science of his society as though they were external to him; they are in him—though in different forms from those in which they appear in the leaders of culture. He cannot rid himself of political beliefs and economic customs by rejecting the more or less external institutions; these customs and beliefs have taken up residence in his mind."[10]

Man is, as Niebuhr suggested, saturated in culture, but the pope identifies a lack of popular awareness of the cultural dimension, a shortcoming he clearly sees as significant. He writes of "artificial consumption," "the spiritual void brought about by atheism," the alienation of men and societies, the manipulation of mass media, and the resulting "*consumer attitudes* and *life-styles*" that "are objectively improper and often damaging to the person's physical and spiritual health."[11] He perceives that even though culture is engraved on the life of each individual and each society, it is difficult to assess its character and impact. As T. S. Eliot observed, "Culture can never be wholly conscious—there is always more to it than we are conscious of; and it cannot be planned because it is also the unconscious background of all our planning."[12] For better or worse, a natural consequence of social life is a lack of awareness of the cultural dimension a person inhabits.

But this is not to say that man is *determined by* his surroundings. He is, rather, conditioned by culture, in both positive and negative ways. As the pope writes, man is "conditioned by the social structure in which he lives, by the education he has received and by his environment." To be sure, a society can be alienated "if its forms of social organization, production and consumption make it more difficult to offer the gift of self and to establish solidarity between people." There is, however, a remedy for this alienation: "a change of lifestyles, of models of production and consumption, and of the established structures of power which today govern societies." Elsewhere John Paul adds: *"A great deal of educational and cultural work* is urgently needed, including the education of consumers in the responsible use of their power of choice, the formation of a strong sense of responsibility among producers and among people in the mass media in particular, as well as the necessary intervention by public authorities."[13]

The pope's approach implicitly acknowledges the autonomy and primacy that culture has attained over the other domains of life. This development is essential to the discussion at hand.

Culture has achieved this special status because, for more than one hundred years, what was new and original determined what was victorious and dominant. This idea, derived from the ubiquitous "belief in progress" that has encompassed our civilization since the Enlightenment,[14] has also been present in economics, politics, and technology. But innovations in these fields are limited—owing, in the case of technology and economics, to available resources and investment costs, and in politics, to institutional structures, control by the opposition, and social tradition. Culture, by contrast, does not face such limits. As a result, cultural elites constantly seek new experiences and sensibilities. Daniel Bell, who thoroughly analyzes how art assumed the role of "storm trooper" or avant-garde, writes in *The Cultural Contradictions of Capitalism*: "What is singular about this 'tradition of the new' (as Harold Rosenberg has called it) is that it allows art to be unfettered, to break down all genres and to explore all modes of experience and sensation. Fantasy today has few costs (is anything deemed bizarre or opprobrious today?) other than the risk of individual madness. And even madness, in the writings of such social theorists as Michel Foucault and R. D. Laing, is now conceived to be a superior form of truth!"[15]

There are four reasons why the primacy of culture in Western civilization is so important. First, it supports John Paul's thesis on the anteriority of culture and the superiority of the spiritual element over economics and politics. Second, the modern culture, which has eliminated questions about truth, the mystery of God, and the identity of man, stands at odds with the papal vision. Third, the "tradition of the new" is not limited to artistic and cultural elites but ends up spreading throughout society, "transforming the thinking and actions of larger masses of people," as Bell puts it.[16] Fourth, the cultural changes in modern life have provoked a structural tension between culture and society's structures (economic, scientific, technological, and, to a lesser degree, political). This tension leads to a sort of schizophrenia in human life, as Bell aptly notes: "On the one hand, the business corporation wants an individual to work hard, pursue a career, accept delayed gratification—to be, in the crude sense, an organization man. And yet, in its products and its advertisements, the corporation promotes pleasure, instant joy, relaxing and letting go. . . . This is self-fulfillment and self-realization!" Elsewhere Bell refers to "the radical disjunction between the social structure (the techno-economic order) and the culture." He explains, "The former is ruled by an economic principle defined in terms of efficiency and functional rationality, the organization of production through the ordering of things, including men as things. The latter is prodigal, promiscuous, dominated by an anti-rational, anti-intellectual temper in which the self is taken as the touchstone of cultural judgments, and the effect on the self is the measure of the aesthetic worth of experience."[17]

Bell's comments anticipate, and help illuminate, the papal critique of economism. Economism generates a simulacrum of culture that leads to what Bell calls "pop hedonism"—or what the pope refers to as "consumerism."

But John Paul makes clear that culture, properly understood, is above all the space where man seeks answers to the most fundamental questions—the questions of meaning and identity.[18] The pope observes that "different cultures are basically different ways of facing the question of the meaning of personal existence," and "every individual must give this response."[19] Accenting the existential and personalist dimension of culture, he quotes the teaching of Vatican II that man is "the only creature on earth that God has wanted for its own sake."[20] Moreover, citing his own encyclical *Redemptor Hominis,* John Paul states: "We are not dealing here with man in the 'abstract,' but with the real, 'concrete,' 'historical' man. We are dealing with *each individual.*" Each human being is endowed with "subjectivity" and is an "autonomous subject of moral decision."[21]

Beyond all that, man's existential quest actually represents the quintessence of culture, because "when this question is eliminated, the culture and moral life of nations are corrupted." In other words, the existential and personalist dimension of culture is inextricably linked to its social dimension. The "social nature of man" finds its outlet primarily in the family and other mediating institutions. In fact, these "economic, social, political and cultural groups . . . stem from human nature itself and have their own autonomy."[22] This sphere is thus the domain of freedom and permits genuine human development.

Troubles arise when the state intrudes on this sphere, John Paul warns. Indeed, the state bears most of the blame for transforming culture's vital particularities into nationalisms, chauvinisms, or, more generally, ideologies. When the state interferes in the "social tissue," culture becomes an instrument in the hands of politics, which infringes on the "subjectivity of society."[23] A state whose goal is the good of its citizens cannot take command of culture, for "the individual today is often suffocated between two poles represented by the State and the marketplace," which reduce him to either a "producer and consumer of goods, or an object of State administration."[24] Culture, as a more fundamental sphere, should not only bestow meaning on those two poles but should also fill the space between them. As one scholar of John Paul's thought put it, "Neither *homo technicus,* nor *homo oeconomicus,* nor *homo politicus* is the pastoral object of the Magisterium, but rather *homo humanus.*"[25]

After noting contemporary society's unfortunate tendency to become "an anonymous and impersonal mass," the pope states that "man remains above all a being who seeks the truth and strives to live in that truth, deepening his understanding of it through a dialogue which involves past and future generations." He continues, "From this open search for truth, which is renewed in every genera- tion, *the culture of a nation* derives its character."[26]

John Paul's is not a static vision of culture. The search for truth always leads to internal challenges and to confrontation with other cultures. "Indeed," the pope observes, "the heritage of values which has been received and handed down is always challenged by the young. To challenge does not necessarily mean to destroy or reject *a priori*, but above all to put these values to test in one's own life, and through this existential verification to make them more real, relevant and personal, distinguishing the valid elements in the tradition from false and erroneous ones, or from obsolete forms." Openness and dialogue are inte- gral parts of a living culture. For "when a culture becomes inward-looking, and tries to perpetuate obsolete ways of living by rejecting any exchange or debate with regard to the truth about man, then it becomes sterile and is heading for decadence."[27]

No discussion of the papal vision of culture would be complete without considering the theological dimension. Both the existential and the social dimensions of culture find their culmination in theological truth. Recall the pope's declaration that "at the heart of every culture lies the attitude man takes to the greatest mystery: the mys- tery of God." Facing the mystery of God and the mystery of transcendence, man draws nearer to the answer to the question about his own identity: "It is through the free gift of self that one truly finds oneself. This gift is made possible by the human person's essential 'capacity for transcendence.' Man cannot give himself to a purely human plan for reality, to an abstract ideal or to a false utopia. As a person, he can give himself to another person or to other persons, and ultimately to God, who is the author of our being and who alone can fully accept our gift."[28] In fact, man, the "spiritual subject," to use the words of Hans Urs von Balthasar, is conscious of his existence and of the fact *that* he is; he is not, however, certain of *what* he is. The answer to the question of identity, of *self-being,* can be found only by submitting oneself to an Absolute. Von Balthasar rightly underscores that certainty about who man "can be provided neither by the nonpersonal, empirical world nor by our fellow men—each of whom can only give questionable and precarious assurances to the other." Rather, such certainty "can only be given by the absolute subject, God."[29]

Hence it is God, the author of man's existence, who reveals its meaning, for he is the end of each man and of each "authentic human community oriented toward his final destiny, which is God." Consequently, "the apex of [human] development is the exercise of the right and duty to seek God, to know him and to live in accordance with that knowledge."[30]

Here, then, we arrive at the definition of culture that *Centesimus Annus* suggests: Culture is the process by which individuals and groups—in particular the family and society—maintain and develop identity, a process driven by the subjectivity inherent in the dignity God bestows on man to pursue the true and the good in dialogue with others.

THE VISION OF MAN IN CENTESIMUS ANNUS

Ultimately, John Paul's whole discussion—whether on political order, the economy, or culture—focuses on anthropology. At the root of the pope's anthropology is undoubtedly the *dignity* of the person. This term appears numerous times in the pages of the encyclical.[31] The dignity of the person stems from the fact that man carries the image of God within himself. As the *imago Dei*, he holds a privileged place in the order of creation because he is "the only creature on Earth which God willed for itself" (a tenet of faith John Paul twice underscores). As a result, faith alone can fully reveal to him his supernatural dignity and his fundamental identity.[32]

By the same token, "the denial of God deprives the person of his foundation," because it "deprives man of one of his basic dimensions, namely the spiritual one." Atheism leads to a "spiritual void,"[33] alienation, and a propensity to degrade the human and natural environment. The pope writes, "Instead of carrying out his role as a cooperator with God in the work of creation, man sets himself up in place of God and thus ends up provoking a rebellion on the part of nature, which is more tyrannized than governed by him. In all this, one notes first the poverty or narrowness of man's outlook, motivated as he is by a desire to possess things rather than to relate them to the truth."[34]

This relation to truth is the essential aspect of John Paul's anthropology. Recall his statement that *"above all"* a man is "a being who seeks the truth and strives to live in that truth, deepening his understanding of it." Elsewhere in the encyclical he describes man as "striving to bear witness to the truth."[35]

Of course, faith in an absolute truth comes into conflict with much of contemporary Western culture. A major social problem has emerged, especially among the intellectual elite and in legal systems, school curricula, and the media. One could say that the problem exists in two forms: a moderate agnosticism that deems belief in absolute truth to be socially perilous, and a radical, ideological agnosticism that repudiates the existence of truth itself.

Polish sociologist Jerzy Szacki offers an example of the *soft* version of this problem: "I consider belief in the absolute as simply menacing. Those touched by this belief (and history provides us with abundant pertinent examples) tend towards an inhuman improvidence, choosing any means which are to lead them to their goal, paying any price in social accounts of losses and gains, and thus minimizing the reality of the goal itself. That is one component. Additionally, fascination with the absolute kills the awareness, required of any active human being, that there are few choices in life which can be made once and forever, thus eliminating the necessity of making choices in the future."[36]

Advocates of such a view above all need to be shown the difference between faith and ideology, as delineated in chapter 2. They must also be reminded of the anti-ideological, anti-utopian, and pluralistic character of the social solutions the pope recommends to the Church, as well as his affirmation that "the Church's method is always that of respect for freedom." John Paul writes, "Total recognition must be given to *the rights of human conscience*, which is bound only to the truth, both natural and revealed. The recognition of these rights represents the primary foundation of every authentically free political order."[37]

The truth about which the pope so often speaks is, then, "the truth of conscience." Contra Szacki, this truth does not eliminate "the necessity of making choices in the future," nor does it extinguish man's liberty, for it is constantly being discovered and continually deepened in dialogue with others. Furthermore, it does not include—let us say it again—a definitive answer regarding how social life should be shaped.

How are we to define the term *truth?* The thrust of the pope's arguments suggests that he means an anthropological truth, particularly since he employs "the truth about man" interchangeably with "truth."[38] Numerous times he asserts the principle that each man possesses a transcendent personal dignity and that therefore an individual cannot be treated in a merely instrumental manner. This truth is rooted in the Revelation brought to the world by Jesus Christ.[39]

The way in which John Paul speaks of this rootedness is fundamental: "No authentic progress is possible without respect for the natural and fundamental right to know the truth and live according to that truth. The exercise and development of this right includes the right to discover and freely to accept Jesus Christ, who is man's true good."[40] Again contra Szacki, no one can *impose* the truth on a person, because each person has the inalienable right to learn the truth, and the reception of Christ must be made "freely." The entire encyclical is studded with accents on the importance and untouchable character of human freedom.

Still, the question remains, would an anthropology of truth based on human dignity be truly dangerous, socially speaking? A related question is, How else can one rationally justify the truth about the dignity of man? Philosopher Nikolaus Lobkowicz cautiously ventures, "Many plead in favor of the hypothesis that the doctrine of the inviolable dignity of man is not very well defended and still less justifies the certitude that God created the human person."[41] From the Enlightenment until the twentieth century, the anthropological solution was, to tell the truth, strongly in vogue. Enlightenment thinkers treated man as an exceptional creature in the cosmos and went so far as to believe that faith in an Absolute debased human greatness and dignity. Nevertheless, as Leszek Kołakowski aptly observed, "To any anthropocentric notion of the world may be objected what the rationalists say about religious belief: that such a notion is nothing but an imaginary contrivance to compensate man's well-justified and depressing awareness of his own infirmity, frailty, uncertainty, finitude."[42] The twentieth century, the century of ideology, proved this view correct. The exhaustion of Enlightenment and scientistic optimism and the confrontation with cultures that deny man his personal dignity, and hence his individual liberty and his rights, seriously challenge Western culture's indifference to the question of the source of human dignity.

Indeed, the "moderate" stance that is afraid to believe in the existence of absolute truth yet dares not to deny its existence categorically either amounts to a disguised form of the radical view that denies the very existence of truth or is a confession of intellectual incoherence. The rejection of the existence of an absolute truth means the negation of the truth as such in human life. As Czech philosopher Jan Patočka observes, the sense of things is not possible as a relative and fragmentary sense of each individual case. Each particular sense refers to the sense of the whole; each relative sense refers to the absolute sense.[43] Kołakowski concludes: "The absence of God, when consistently upheld and thoroughly examined, spells the ruin of man in the sense that it demolishes or robs of meaning everything we have been used to think of as the essence of being human: the quest for truth, the distinction of good and evil, the claim to dignity, the claim to creating something that withstands the indifferent destructiveness of time."[44]

John Paul's explication of anthropological truth rooted in the dignity that God bestows on man illuminates the two dimensions of human transcendence, vertical (the personal bond between man and God) and horizontal (man's transcendence over the world of things). Man, as a subject endowed with freedom and intelligence, surpasses the material world but also expresses himself and realizes himself through creative work in that world.[45]

The pope perceives human life as a multidimensional and creative, with individual and social growth coming through the gift of self to others and to God.[46] Writing in the Italian journal *La Società*, Mariano Fazio notes, "John Paul II accents a vision of the human person in which the ontological structure is open towards God and others. In the metaphysical transcendence of the person, that is, in the real transcendence of the self, the vocation of man is fulfilled."[47] Man, in short, is called to love.

Man's fulfillment through love is derived from, and the deepest expression of, his social nature—something that both collectivism and individualism corrode, as the pope stresses. In making the gift of self, man is capable of "entering into that relationship of solidarity and communion with others for which God created him," John Paul writes. This capacity often finds expression in collaboration with other human beings—be it in the economic sphere, where man acts by inserting himself "in a progressively expanding chain of solidarity," or the political sphere, where through "dialogue and solidarity" people seek a social order "free of oppression and based on a spirit of cooperation and solidarity." This is why the pope states that "openness to dialogue and to cooperation is required of all people of good will, and in particular of individuals and groups with specific responsibilities in the areas of politics, economics and social life, at both the national and international levels."[48]

Dialogue and *solidarity*: these words are key to the vision of social life outlined in *Centesimus Annus*. Dialogue is a method of realizing the common good as well as discovering the truth; it is also a way of building interpersonal ties. Solidarity, or social love, is a principle that forbids neglecting or excluding a man or a group of people, or for that matter favoring a certain person or group—a point Pope Leo XIII made in *Rerum Novarum*.[49] From this principle follows a "preferential option for the poor," which John Paul defines (citing his own words from *Sollicitudo Rei Socialis*) as a "special form of primacy in the exercise of Christian charity." He adds, "This option is not limited to material poverty, since it is well known that there are many other forms of poverty, especially in modern society—not only economic but cultural and spiritual poverty as well."[50]

This vision of the person could appear somewhat

idealistic if the pope did not complement it with an explanation of the fissure caused by sin. This fissure is present in
everyone, for each man "bears within himself the wound
of original sin, which constantly draws him toward evil."
John Paul explains, "Not only is *this doctrine an integral
part of Christian revelation*, it also has great hermeneutic
value insofar as it helps one to understand human reality. Man tends toward good, but he is also capable of evil.
He can transcend his immediate interest and still remain
bound to it." Bearing the wound of original sin, each man
stands in need of the Redemption.[51]

THE PLACE OF ANTHROPOLOGY
IN CENTESIMUS ANNUS

Given the importance of John Paul's vision of man in
Centesimus Annus, we must consider the problem of
anthropology itself. What is its relationship with theology
and Catholic social teaching? What crucial themes about
the nature of man does it touch upon?

John Paul clearly establishes anthropology as the
framework of the Church's social doctrine. Reflecting on
Rerum Novarum, he writes, "It will be necessary to keep
in mind that the main thread and, in a certain sense, the
guiding principle of Pope Leo's Encyclical, and of all the
Church's social doctrine, is *a correct view of the human person* and of his unique value." Later he adds that the obligation of the Church's social teaching is "to incarnate the
one truth about man in different and constantly changing
social, economic and political contexts." Underscoring the

importance of anthropology, the pope states, "Christian anthropology therefore is really a chapter of theology, and for this reason, the Church's social doctrine, by its concern for man and by its interest in him and in the way he conducts himself in the world, 'belongs to the field . . . of theology and particularly of moral theology.' "[52]

An interest in man himself should be interpreted primarily as a call to think about the essence of the human person as well as his condition. The emphasis on human acts guides our attention to the human milieu—above all, the moral milieu, of which the pope speaks when he addresses the great significance of "human ecology."[53]

Here one arrives at another question: Is the anthropology professed by the pope an anthropology of *man* or an anthropology of *men*? That is, does it see a being of universal and unchanging nature or those myriad individuals who make up the human race?

It is difficult to give an unequivocal answer. On the one hand, John Paul strongly states that the Church is dealing not with the abstract but with the concrete person immersed in history. On the other hand, the truth about man he discusses is of a universal character. There is no doubt that man realizes himself in society, through belonging to various communities and in contacts with other people. At the same, the Church is "opposed to models in which the individual is lost in the crowd, in which the role of his initiative and freedom is neglected." The pope touches on the tension when he writes, "Man receives from God his essential dignity and with it the capacity to transcend every social order so as to move toward truth and goodness. But he is also conditioned by the social structure in which he lives, by the education he has received and by his environment."[54]

How to reconcile these two perspectives? The first response arises from theology. Man is created in the image and likeness of God; as such, human nature does not have to fear social entanglements that simply cannot touch it. The social doctrine of the Church, the pope notes, "proclaims God and his mystery of salvation in Christ to every human being, and for that very reason reveals man to himself. In this light, and only in this light, does it concern itself with everything else: the human rights of the individual, and in particular of the 'working class,' the family and education, the duties of the State, the ordering of national and international society, economic life, culture, war and peace, and respect for life from the moment of conception until death."[55]

The second response hinges on the concepts of truth and freedom. The search for truth is, of course, fundamental: recall John Paul's statement that "man remains above all a being who seeks the truth and strives to live in that truth." At the same time, this search for the truth can and must be realized only within a space of freedom, as we saw in chapter 2.

For John Paul, there is no doubt that the modern world often sets the search for truth and the practice of freedom against each other. Central to his criticism of ideology in all forms is that it separates freedom and truth—and in the process hurts both. Totalitarianisms are doomed to fail because their leaders, convinced that they hold the absolute truth and confident in imposing it on society, eliminate the field of freedom. Human beings will not tolerate this for long. In the end, the pope writes, "not only is it wrong from the ethical point of view to disregard human nature, which is made for freedom, but in practice it is impossible to do so."[56]

But John Paul does not call for the apotheosis of freedom at the price of truth. He very clearly states that "totalitarianism arises out of a denial of truth in the objective sense." The pope adds, "If there is no transcendent truth, in obedience to which man achieves his full identity, then there is no sure principle for guaranteeing just relations between people.[57] . . . If one does not acknowledge transcendent truth, then the force of power takes over, and each person tends to make full use of the means at his disposal." That is why "freedom attains its full development only by accepting the truth. In a world without truth, freedom loses its foundation and man is exposed to the violence of passion and to manipulation, both open and hidden." Elsewhere John Paul writes of the erroneous "understanding of human freedom which detaches it from obedience to the truth, and consequently from the duty to respect the rights of others," an error that easily slides into egoism. Far from submitting itself to freedom, the absolute truth of which the pope writes guarantees that freedom.[58]

In the pope's anthropology, then, man is a creature bound to undertake a free search for truth or, rather, to exercise his freedom in truth. Man possesses not only "the right to freedom" but also "the duty of making responsible use of freedom."[59] Freedom is a necessary condition for the possibility of learning the truth; at the same time, truth protects freedom from degeneration and even from annihilation. Considered separately, freedom and truth can lead to totalitarianism; only their interdependence confers on them an antitotalitarian character.

The social doctrine of the Church (whose foundation is anthropological) should therefore delineate the framework of a sociopolitical system that permits human beings to realize a freedom centered on the truth.

Truth and freedom are intrinsically united at their source—that is, in the acts of Creation and Revelation. These acts allow man to participate in the divine truth and grant him a freedom that is truly liberated from all determinisms. They also recognize the fragmentation of knowledge and the wound original sin inflicted on thought and the will, and thus inscribe man's quest within a space of freedom respectful of the truth.

Two other crucial concepts are linked with truth and freedom: the dignity of the human person and his development. The human person is endowed with dignity in virtue of the divine act of Creation,[60] and this dignity, fully revealed by Christ,[61] belongs primarily to the domain of the truth. This strict dependency of the personal dignity of man on Creation and Revelation is often underestimated, but Romano Guardini explicated the connection: "The personal character of man belongs to his constituent features. One can discern it and accept it morally only that at the moment when, thanks to Revelation, our eyes open on our relation with a living and personal God. This relation is clarified in the fact that we are children of God and that Providence exists. Without this reference, we could speak of a harmonious, subtle, and creative personality, but certainly not of the person as such. For the person is the ultimate measure of man and transcends all psychological or cultural property of the nature. So therefore, the knowledge of the person is bound closely to the Christian faith. The acceptance and the recognition of man as person will survive for a time without doubt the extinction of the faith itself, before having to disappear ineluctably."[62] Human dignity—rooted in a transcendental truth—demands respect. It is a factor that must be taken into consideration in each action and in each social system. John Paul puts the matter concisely: "Every individual—whatever his or her personal convictions—bears the image of God and therefore deserves respect."[63]

The principal aspects of John Paul's anthropology were evident well before he ascended to the papacy. In *The Acting Person* (1969), Karol Wojtyla offered an exhaustive exposition of this view of man. Wojtyla's former student Andrzej Szostek mentions this in describing the pope's understanding of the source of human dignity: "The author here confirms and expands upon a belief often expressed in the philosophical tradition according to which the personal structure is essential to man. It is this which constitutes the ontological basis of his dignity. The 'ratio' of the personal value of man is that which distinguishes him from the world of nature: namely, the fact of being a person manifesting himself by the presence of a spiritual element, in the transcendence and causality proper to the person. What is good for man is that which strengthens and perfects this structure; what is bad for him is what obliterates or ignores it."[64]

Szostek calls attention to a theme of capital importance: the causality of man. This causality stems from the human capability for self-determination—that is, for creating oneself through the activity of will without ever being determined by the object of one's cognition, desires, or aspirations. [65] Human dignity realizes itself in action; as noted earlier, the model of action accomplished by man is work. As John Paul writes, work "belongs to the vocation of every person; indeed, man expresses and fulfills himself by working." Hence work is also one of the principal anthropological categories. A person can express and improve his dignity through his labor, and it is necessary to "restore dignity to work as the free activity of man."[66]

The need to realize oneself in and through work is connected to the anthropological vision of man, created in the image of God, endowed with intelligence and freedom, and profoundly creative by nature. Thus, man must be guaranteed not only freedom but also the possibility of undertaking creative endeavors. This is a fundamental need, and society should be organized to realize that need.

In short, as truth is realized in freedom and freedom has its foundation in truth, so is human dignity realized in creative action, which must constantly take account of the need to respect this dignity. In other words, truth delimits the space of true freedom, and human dignity encircles the frontiers of creative action.

CULTURE AND THE MARKET

At each level of his analysis, John Paul recalls that the truth about God and man, a truth made concrete in the conception of the human person, requires that the best conditions for the development of man be arranged. Thus the anthropological reflections tracked to this point must be complemented by the two following concepts: culture and the market.

In conforming to the mystery of God, culture also conforms itself to the mystery of Revelation, and as a result man has become the depository of the revealed truth. Equally important, culture positions itself with respect to the mystery of divine creation and above all to that of the creation of man, who is "made for freedom."[67] This means that the concept of culture in the Church's social doctrine includes the anthropological categories of truth and freedom. Such an understanding of culture is confirmed in *Centesimus Annus.*

One of the foundations of the papal anthropology is the affirmation that an aspiration for truth is inscribed in the vocation of man. John Paul goes further: "From this open search for truth, which is renewed in every generation, *the culture of a nation* derives its character." The truth is a constitutive part of culture that itself develops in a space of liberty, as the pope suggests when he says that in dialogue with others, the Christian should be attentive to "every fragment of truth which he encounters in the life experience and in the culture of individuals and of nations."[68]

The essential attributes of culture are its openness and its creativity. It develops above all through dialogue. The pope insists on this dialogue and development when he states, "*Evangelization too plays a role in the culture of the various nations,* sustaining culture in its progress toward the truth, and assisting in the work of its purification and enrichment."[69]

Cultural action needs a space of freedom—freedom

for actions respectful of human dignity (and thus respectful of a truth rooted in the transcendent truth of Creation and Redemption). If this indispensable condition is
met, it sanctions the institution of the free market. The
economy is one of the principal domains where diverse
human activities find expression, one of the interdepen-
dent spheres of action and culture. Of course, the market
is not an end in itself, one with its own theological justification. The pope endorses the capitalist economy as it is
capable of fulfilling the needs defined by anthropology.
But we must always remember that primacy goes to the
religious and ethical.

John Paul's qualified approval of the free market is evident in this passage: "The modern *business economy* has
positive aspects. Its basis is human freedom exercised in
the economic field, just as it is exercised in many other
fields. Economic activity is indeed but one sector in a great
variety of human activities, and like every other sector, it
includes the right to freedom, as well as the duty of making
responsible use of freedom." The pope reminds us that the
market should accept and arrange favorable conditions for
the development of human freedom. The market, he says,
finds justification in its providing space for "free human
creativity." Hence it must be a place reserved for the exercise of freedom in respect for truth, a place respectful of
values and human dignity and more fully incarnated in
culture. For the market, like liberty and activity, is not
wholly autonomous: it requires the support of a vigorous
ethical-cultural system. "Of itself, an economic system
does not possess criteria for correctly distinguishing new
and higher forms of satisfying human needs from artificial

new needs which hinder the formation of a mature personality. Thus *a great deal of educational and cultural work* is urgently needed."[70]

Such views are often questioned today, and they were categorically rejected when the modern liberal state was created. In that era, Wilhelm Röpke wrote, many believed "that a competitive market economy, based on division of labor, was an excellent moral academy which, by appealing to their self-interest, encouraged men to be pacific and decent, as well as to practice all the other civic virtues. While we know today—and it could always have been known—that competition reduces the moral stamina and therefore requires moral reserves outside the market economy; at that time they were deluded enough to believe that, on the contrary, it increases the moral stock."[71]

It is a revealing fact that in the second half of the twentieth century, many representatives of neoliberalism came to share Röpke's opinions. One of its most distinguished representatives, Friedrich Hayek, wrote in "The Moral Element in Free Enterprise" that "the system [of free enterprise] is itself only a means, and its infinite possibilities must be used in the service of ends which exist apart." Hayek fingered the inherent contradiction of this system: "A society which has no other standard than efficiency will indeed waste that efficiency."[72]

More and more economists and businesspeople are coming to this view. The center of discussion thus shifts from the problem of whether ethics ought to be present in the economy at all toward reflection on particular values, their origins, and how they should be incorporated into the free market. This shift creates a new opportunity for dialogue between Catholic social doctrine and representatives of the economic world.

In *Centesimus Annus*, John Paul raises an essential point, one on which great work must be done in the field of education and culture to demonstrate: "Even prior to the logic of a fair exchange of goods and the forms of justice appropriate to it, there exists *something which is due to man because he is man*, by reason of his lofty dignity." In other words, in economic life, people acting under free competition must always remember that "there are many human needs which find no place on the market" and some "important human needs which escape its logic."[73]

John Paul's exhortation that actors in the free market remember the market's limitations is not a paternalistic reprimand but rather a reminder that only a system founded on a "correct conception of the human person" can be truly effective in political-economic life. The importance of this idea is a thread that runs through *Centesimus Annus*. The pope observes that socialism collapsed precisely because of an "anthropological error"—namely, "the socialization of man" or "the nationalization of the person." Another type of anthropological error threatens democratic capitalism, he points out: "It is possible for the financial accounts to be in order, and yet for the people—who make up the firm's most valuable asset—to be humiliated and their dignity offended. Besides being morally inadmissible, this will eventually have negative repercussions on the firm's economic efficiency." Similarly, the pope interprets the events of 1989 as "a warning to those who, in the name of political realism, wish to banish law and morality from the political arena."[74]

Just as in the long run one cannot scorn truth with impunity, so one cannot ignore freedom. "Not only is it wrong from the ethical point of view to disregard human nature, which is made for freedom, but in practice it is impossible to do so," John Paul writes. "Where society is so organized as to reduce arbitrarily or even suppress the sphere in which freedom is legitimately exercised, the result is that the life of society becomes progressively disorganized and goes into decline."[75]

There can be no escape from the responsibility to root economic (or political) activity in a culture founded on a "correct conception of the human person," an anthropology *Centesimus Annus* brings to light. There can be no market without a culture, just as there can be no freedom without truth, no action and initiative without respect for freedom and human dignity.

That is why the Church's social doctrine aims, among other things, to indicate those political structures that permit fruitful connection and mediation between culture and the sphere of action. This is the source of John Paul's qualified praise for democracy and for the market. But the concern of social doctrine is to return to the market and democracy their foundation in culture, one based on recognition of the personal dignity of man.

TRANSCENDENTAL TRUTH AND HUMAN DIGNITY

To summarize, the act of Creation endowed man with an unlimited dignity, manifesting itself and perfecting itself in action, and has called him to creative initiative.

The Redemption of humanity brought by Jesus Christ has revealed, in a very special way, the personal dignity of each man, as well as a freedom transcending all determinism.[76] Thus man "is made for freedom," which is a prerequisite for his creative work and his spirit of enterprise. But he is obliged to use liberty in a way that respects the truth, of which divine Revelation has made man the depository. To man, wounded by original sin, that truth—which concerns the way of salvation, not social solutions—is necessarily fragmented. Man, and the Church, must continually examine and consider this truth.

Transcendental truth and human dignity find their reflection in culture, while action—that is, economics and politics—should open up a space in which to realize the values contained in this culture. Has not the author of *Centesimus Annus* time and again insisted on an "authentic theology of integral human liberation" and on the "integral development of the human person," and stressed that "development must not be understood solely in economic terms, but in a way that is fully human"?[77] The development of man and the growth of his community should be, by their nature, holistic; the development of one fragment becomes a deformation. This development is realized, Pope John Paul II emphasizes, in a life offered to others, a life of love—that is to say, in the voluntary gift of oneself to God and to men.

FROM CENTESIMUS ANNUS TO CARITAS IN VERITATE

In 2009, Pope John Paul II's successor, Benedict XVI, issued a new social encyclical, *Caritas in Veritate* (Charity in Truth). As Benedict's first social encyclical—and the Holy See's first social encyclical since *Centesimus Annus* eighteen years earlier—*Caritas in Veritate* was awaited with great anticipation. Adding to the interest was the fact that the encyclical was issued in the midst of a global recession.

Perhaps the most notable aspect of *Caritas in Veritate* is its ambiguities and tensions. In many ways Benedict's encyclical evokes the spirit not of its immediate predecessor, *Centesimus Annus*, but rather of Pope Paul VI's *Populorum Progressio* (1967). Benedict even calls *Populorum Progressio* (which, as we saw in chapter 1, was marked by imprecise criticisms of the market economy) "the *Rerum Novarum* of the present age, shedding light upon humanity's journey towards unity."[1] At the same time, however,

Benedict frequently cites *Centesimus Annus* and is clearly indebted to the vision John Paul II laid out in that encyclical. As such, Benedict's encyclical demonstrates the ongoing impact of John Paul's contribution to Catholic social teaching.

CARITAS IN VERITATE

Caritas in Veritate is a wide-ranging encyclical. It deals with financial crisis and technological development, ecology and bioethics, civil society and abortion, the relationship between faith and reason, the social responsibility of business, in vitro fertilization and globalization, business enterprise and demographic problems, and more. Although covering such a wide spectrum of topics enables Benedict to depict the complexity of the modern world, it means that each subject can be touched on only briefly rather than discussed thoroughly. The encyclical also highlights tensions and contradictions within the globalizing economies, and in fact it is marked by tensions of its own. Therefore, as a statement on man's place within the culture, and in particular within economic and political systems, *Caritas in Veritate* lacks the coherence displayed in *Centesimus Annus*.

Some of the differences between *Caritas in Veritate* and *Centesimus Annus* stem from how Benedict and John Paul view Catholic social teaching. John Paul strongly emphasizes that the social teaching of the Church should be neither a "third way" nor an ideology. It should aim instead at directing human action, and therefore it belongs mainly to the field of moral theology. In *Sollicitudo Rei Socialis,* John Paul describes the Church's social doctrine as "the accurate formulation of the results of a careful reflection on the complex realities of human existence, in society and in the international order, in the light of faith and of the Church's tradition."[2] Benedict, however, treats the Church's social teaching in a much more general and pastoral manner. In *Caritas* he mentions the teaching only once, when he defines it as "*caritas in veritate in re sociali*: the proclamation of the truth of Christ's love in society."[3]

According to Benedict, the main problem humanity faces today is globalization. John Paul made a similar point in *Laborem Exercens,* but twenty-eight years after *Laborem,* some of the cultural, political, and economical implications of globalization have become more clearly defined.

Benedict identifies two cultural dangers associated with globalization. One is *cultural eclecticism,* by which "cultures are simply placed alongside one another and viewed as substantially equivalent and interchangeable." As a result, there is "no authentic dialogue and therefore . . . no true integration" among cultures. The second danger is *cultural leveling,* which is marked by "indiscriminate acceptance of types of conduct and life-styles." This danger leads to the opposite problem: "One loses sight of the profound significance of the culture of different nations, of the traditions of the various peoples, by which the individual defines himself in relation to life's fundamental questions."[4]

According to Benedict, the main political issue with globalization involves "the limitations to [a country's] sovereignty imposed by the new context of international

trade and finance." The main economic problem, meanwhile, results from the fact that a globalizing market "has
stimulated first and foremost, on the part of rich countries,
a search for areas in which to outsource production at low
cost." Benedict chronicles the dangerous consequences of
this phenomenon: "These processes have led to a downsiz-
ing of social security systems as the price to be paid for
seeking a greater competitive advantage in the global market, with consequent grave danger for the rights of workers, for fundamental human rights and for the solidarity
associated with the traditional forms of the social State."[5]

The pope rightly claims that the global economic crisis
resulted primarily from irresponsible activity on the part
of those who shape the world economy. He also argues
that it stemmed from difficult-to-define "technical forces"
and "global interrelations": "The technical forces in play,
the global interrelations, the damaging effects on the real
economy of badly managed and largely speculative financial dealings, large-scale migration of people, often provoked by some particular circumstances and then given
insufficient attention, the unregulated exploitation of the
earth's resources: all this leads us today to reflect on the
measures that would be necessary to provide a solution."[6]

But offsetting these criticisms of the global market
economy are passages highlighting positive aspects of globalization. In one passage the pope writes that the process
of globalization, "originating within economically developed countries," spread through all economies and "has
been the principal driving force behind the emergence
from underdevelopment of whole regions." He adds that
globalization thus "represents a great opportunity." To take

another example, Benedict recognizes that "the export of investments and skills can benefit the population of the receiving country."[7]

His opinion of business enterprise is similarly ambivalent. On one hand, he takes a critical approach to it: "Today's international economic scene, marked by grave deviations and failures, requires a profound new way of understanding business enterprise. Without doubt, one of the greatest risks for businesses is that they are almost exclusively answerable to their investors." On the other hand, he sees positive signs in the way some business leaders understand their social responsibility: "There is nevertheless a growing conviction that business management cannot concern itself only with the interests of the proprietors, but must also assume responsibility for the other stakeholders who contribute to the life of the business: the workers, the clients, the suppliers of various elements of production, the community of reference."[8]

Much the same attitude is evident in Benedict's treatment of trade unions. The pope affirms the validity of trade unions' mission to protect workers' rights in an environment he describes as often hostile to those unions: "Through the combination of social and economic change, trade union organizations experience greater difficulty in carrying out their task of representing the interests of workers, partly because governments, for reasons of economic utility, often limit the freedom or the negotiating capacity of labor unions. Hence traditional networks of solidarity have more and more obstacles to overcome. The repeated calls issued within the Church's social doctrine, beginning with *Rerum Novarum,* for the promotion of workers' associations that can defend their rights must therefore be honored today even more than in the past." Yet after offering this strong endorsement of labor unions, the pope notes that they "tend to limit themselves to defending the interests of their registered members" and urges them to "turn their attention to those outside their membership."[9]

Benedict's basic premise, often repeated in the encyclical, is that we ought to make love present in all areas of social life. He does not analyze reasons for the complex cultural, political, and economic issues he identifies or offer specific solutions from within modern systems. In fact, the encyclical states explicitly that "the Church does not have technical solutions to offer."[10] He recommends a general search for new political ideas and new social and economic systems—which leads, ultimately, to an appeal for radical change in modern culture, economy, and politics.

Notably, Benedict's suggestions for change often take the form of demands: "is required," "requires changes," "shall be avoided," or "one shall." The pope declares, for example, that the worldwide economic crisis "obliges us" to "set ourselves new rules and to discover new forms of commitment" as well as "new solutions." Elsewhere he states, "Today's international economic scene, marked by grave deviations and failures, requires a profound change." Hence "a new trajectory of thinking is needed"; "there is a need for men in search of a new humanism"; and the political power shall aim at "the process of constructing a new order of economic productivity."[11] In many cases the breadth of the pope's demands raises questions about whether it is possible to achieve the solutions.[12]

Concerning the economy, *Caritas in Veritate* is often

in accord with *Centesimus Annus*. That is to say, Benedict generally praises the market as "the economic institution that permits an encounter between persons, inasmuch as they are economic subjects," while firmly warning against both "autonomous economy" and the "application of commercial logic" in other areas of life. But his assessment of the modern economy is somewhat more negative than John Paul's, and some of his suggestions are both far-reaching and vague. He writes, for instance, "All in all, what is needed is a specific and profound form of economic democracy"—a market that permits, in conditions of equal opportunity, the free operation of (1) private enterprises, (2) public enterprises, and (3) those enterprises that "pursue social goals and mutual help." Benedict claims that the development of this market should be a constraint-free process, and yet elsewhere he seems to praise economic interventionism at both national and global levels (without providing much detail as to what that interventionism would look like). Given the vagueness and inconsistencies in the encyclical, *Caritas in Veritas* reintroduces (wittingly or unwittingly) the prospect of a "third way" economic approach as part of the Church's social teaching.[13]

What we particularly need, Benedict asserts, "is a worldwide redistribution of energy resources."[14] Here we come to the encyclical's most controversial passage:

> *To manage the global economy; to revive economies hit by the crisis; to avoid any deterioration of the present crisis and the greater imbalances that would result; to bring about integral and timely disarmament, food security and peace; to guarantee the protection of the*

environment and to regulate migration: for all this, there is urgent need of a true world political authority, as my predecessor Blessed John XXIII indicated some years ago. Such an authority would need to be regulated by law, to observe consistently the principles of subsidiarity and solidarity, to seek to establish the common good, and *to make a commitment to securing authentic integral human development inspired by the values of charity in truth.* Furthermore, such an authority would need to be universally recognized and to be vested with the effective power to ensure security for all, regard for justice, and respect for rights. Obviously it would have to have the authority to ensure compliance with its decisions from all parties, and also with the coordinated measures adopted in various international forums. Without this, despite the great progress accomplished in various sectors, international law would risk being conditioned by the balance of power among the strongest nations.[15]

According to the pope, such a "world political authority" would manage the global economy, conduct a common disarmament program, protect world peace and the environment, and regulate worldwide migration. It should abide by the rules of subsidiarity, solidarity, and the common good, be regulated by law, and operate in accord with the idea of charity in truth. What's more, it should be recognized by all the countries of the globe and should enjoy such power that it could act efficiently to enforce the fulfillment of obligations.

Unfortunately, this ideal is as far from being fulfilled as it was when the first utopian socialists put forward similar fine postulates two hundred years ago.

Even here, contradictions are apparent. While taking a maximalist approach to global political power, Benedict criticizes the "actual effectiveness" of international organizations, noting that their "bureaucratic and administrative machinery" is "excessively costly." He suggests "a more devolved and organic, less bureaucratic" system of social solidarity both within national boundaries and internationally. Benedict's emphasis on subsidiarity and the importance of a civil society puts him more clearly in line with his papal predecessors, including John Paul II. He observes that the creation of civil society has led to increased citizen participation in politics and that it is in civil society where the economy of gratuitousness and fraternity may develop. Echoing John Paul's statement that man's social nature is "realized in various intermediary groups," Benedict writes that "the autonomy of intermediate bodies . . . fosters freedom and participation through assumption of responsibility" and is "the most effective antidote against any form" of paternalism. Similarly, the pope sounds a realistic tone when he reminds us of the close link between individual rights and duties in both wealthy societies and societies in need.[16]

Many commentators have remarked on the challenges that come with understanding an encyclical that only touches on so many complex issues. Baylor University philosophy professor Thomas S. Hibbs commented on "the document's dizzying capaciousness, the way it seems to want to discuss everything and embrace almost everything, even things that seem on the surface incompatible." He pointed out that largely because *Caritas in Veritate* "does not say enough about the nature of the common good," it "leaves us guessing a bit as to the principles needed to spell out the relationship" between subsidiarity and globalism.[17]

George Weigel, Pope John Paul II's biographer, seized on the tensions inherent in *Caritas in Veritate.* The encyclical "seems to be a hybrid," he wrote, "blending the pope's own insightful thinking on the social order with elements of the [Pontifical Council for] Justice and Peace approach to Catholic social doctrine, which imagines that doctrine beginning anew at *Populorum Progressio.*" Weigel went so far as to say that the encyclical "resembles a duck-billed platypus."[18]

But even these commentators acknowledge areas of continuity with John Paul's *Centesimus Annus* and the longer line of papal social teaching. Weigel highlights many crucial insights in *Caritas in Veritate*—on issues ranging from the causes of Third World poverty to the impact of low birthrates on the global economy to the link between religious freedom and economic development—that run "in continuity with John Paul II and his extension of the line of papal argument inspired by *Rerum Novarum* in *Centesimus Annus.*"[19]

Like John Paul, Benedict also writes persuasively about the dangers of ideology. As we have seen, criticism of ideologies of all kinds is central to John Paul's case in *Centesimus Annus.* In *Caritas in Veritate,* Benedict writes of "the *danger constituted by utopian and ideological visions.*" Later he affirms the need "to liberate ourselves from ideologies, which often oversimplify reality in artificial ways," and calls on us "to examine objectively the full human dimension of the problems."[20]

Although Benedict hardly mentions specific political solutions in his social encyclical, one can conclude that, like John Paul, he considers the democratic rule of law to be the best political system. Benedict stresses the fact that although different forms of the state are permissible, we should always reinforce "the guarantees proper to the *State of law*: a system of public order and effective imprisonment that respects human rights, truly democratic institutions." Moreover, he emphasizes that an increase in poverty "places democracy at risk."[21]

But the most important area of overlap involves the nature of the human person. Benedict writes repeatedly of "integral human development." As Joseph Fessio, SJ, puts it, the pope makes integral human development "the centerpiece of the Church's social teaching." Notre Dame law professor Richard Garnett writes, "In keeping with the Catholic social teaching tradition, and with the work of his predecessor, the letter is about *the person*—about who we are and why it matters. Beneath, and supporting, the various statements and suggestions regarding specific policy questions is the bedrock of Christian moral anthropology, of the good news about the dignity, vocation, and destiny of man."[22]

In this way, *Caritas in Veritate* is, as Weigel rightly observes, an "extension of John Paul II's signature theme"—namely, "that all social issues, including political and economic questions, are ultimately questions of the nature of the human person."[23] Thus, even as Benedict's social encyclical cites, and evokes the spirit of, earlier encyclicals—especially *Populorum Progressio*—it also builds on the work of Pope John Paul II. This connection demonstrates the fundamental continuity in Catholic social teaching and reaffirms that *Centesimus Annus* will remain an essential and irremovable link in the chain from *Rerum Novarum* to future social encyclicals.

THE IRREVERSIBLE CONTRIBUTION OF CENTESIMUS ANNUS

Continuity in the teaching of the popes is a point on which John Paul insists in *Centesimus Annus.* The very circumstances surrounding the writing of the encyclical make the point: it was published to commemorate the hundredth anniversary of *Rerum Novarum* and included many citations drawn from encyclicals published during the intervening century.

But we cannot stop at acknowledging how *Centesimus Annus* is in keeping with the earlier social encyclicals on economic and political life. To do so would be to overlook the crucial contributions John Paul makes in this encyclical. By alluding to the "new things" occurring at the end of the twentieth century, and by taking an original approach to the theme, John Paul reaches beyond the usual range of Catholic teaching. That is why it is essential to understand the vision the pope sketches in *Centesimus Annus.*

One contribution of *Centesimus Annus* is to return to an integral (which does not mean a systematic or total) perception of social reality, a vision announced in *Rerum Novarum* and *Quadragesimo Anno.* Other social encyclicals were sometimes inclined to furnish abstract analyses, which were susceptible to ideological distortion and which subjected the pontifical documents to a nearly unlimited freedom of interpretation.

That integral vision is based on "methodological anthropocentrism," which is the most important factor to consider with *Centesimus Annus*. The pope's focus on the truth about man as a person is fundamental for the Church's social teaching for four reasons:

First, in focusing its reflections on man and social life, methodological anthropocentrism constructs a broad platform common to Catholics and to people of other faiths and worldviews. It also opens new possibilities for dialogue—and even confrontation—with contemporary social thought.

Second, this anthropological approach in effect frees Church teaching from historical entanglements that have incited sentiments of distrust toward modern liberal democracy. (The release of the Syllabus of Errors in 1864—condemning various philosophies and religious attitudes that had become prevalent post-Enlightenment—suggests the hostility that could develop between the Church and broader society.) Through the prism of anthropology, it is much easier to see that the fundamental institutions of democratic capitalism are a product of Christian culture, built on Christian terrain. This recognition weakens the thesis, previously honored within the Church, that the institutions are intrinsically amoral and incompatible with the Gospel.

Third, anthropology reinserts the *person* into the world of democratic institutions and the market economy. The person—endowed with a transcendent dignity though wounded by sin—is capable of fulfillment through an active solidarity and a creative use of his abilities and his intelligence. Anthropology avoids an ideological description of political and economic reality and reorients the Church's engagement with public life. It allows the Church to recognize that democratic politics and a market economy can create a place favorable to realizing a Christian vocation and to having a substantive debate on the common good and the means of achieving it.

Fourth, the pope's use of anthropology requires an adjustment in the Church's assessment of socialism. The promises of socialist theorists have rung sweetly in some Christian ears,[24] but an anthropological perspective sheds light on socialism's fundamental error: the way it subordinates the person to the larger socialist system, removing the autonomy of the person and the subjectivity of society. By offering this diagnosis and sifting the concrete manifestations of capitalist reality, *Centesimus Annus* is saved from the temptations of statism and central planning. It also avoids becoming entangled in debates about the possibilities of a Christian socialism or the search for a "third way." Ultimately, these observations underscore the necessity of serious work in the domains of education and culture if we are to prevent the excesses and pathologies engendered by capitalism.[25] *Centesimus Annus* is clear-eyed about the shortcomings of democratic capitalism and the dangers that can arise in such a system. But it demonstrates that the Church's goal is not to design social institutions that would be of a more "confessional" shape; the goal, rather, is to evangelize the human being who lives in the democratic world and labors in the free market.

FAITH VS. IDEOLOGY

Centesimus Annus makes another contribution by introducing a distinction between faith and ideology that had never appeared so clearly in the Church's teaching. This distinction is important for three reasons:

First, the boundary between evangelical and ideological attitudes can be rather fluid, especially because both attitudes claim for themselves an unimpeachable orthodoxy and are characterized by a personal commitment that is sometimes manifested in heroic witness. But there *is* a distinction between them that must be recognized. John Paul introduces this distinction, in the process making the Church sensitive to the necessity of protecting from ideological corruption the deposit of faith that has been confided to it. This also enables a theological critique of religious ideologies. As the eminent theologian Cardinal Walter Kasper wrote: "Whoever considers Christian freedom to be a fundamental liberation from the law in the interest of some utopian society without authority, or whoever uses law as a pretext for destabilizing legal structures, to the extent that they are free and proper structures, and who in this sense, even if it is only a rhetorical one, manufactures revolutionary changes, can rely neither on the Old nor on the New Testament, and not on the testimony of the early, pre-Constantinian Church, either. He has misunderstood the Christian message of freedom and has placed it at the service of alien ideological purposes."[26]

The distinction between faith and ideology helps overcome a dangerous polarization, present in the Church since the Enlightenment, between "integrists and fundamentalists" on the one hand, and "modernists and liberals" on the other. This dichotomy led the attitudes to harden into ideologies and aggravated the antagonism between the two. Thanks to the pope, it is easier to recover the weighty arguments advanced by both camps and to recognize the dangers arising from ideological versions of these attitudes.

Second, the distinction between ideology and faith allows us to show that Christianity by its very nature is not an ideology and that the Church by its very nature has no totalitarian ambitions. The majority of the faithful instinctively understand these points, but many non-Catholics do not. Worse, many fear the Church as a force that aspires to dominate social life. Reinforcing their apprehensions are clichés and widespread cultural stereotypes, along with the voices of the heralds of a Christianity reduced to a fundamentalist ideology. These false prophets are few, to be sure, but with the enemies of Christianity amplifying their distortions, they seriously hinder the Church's evangelical mission.

The distinction between ideology and faith thus clarifies the true nature of the Church by alleviating certain excessive fears and by showing that the Church knows how to identify—and combat—religious fundamentalisms and ideologies.

Third, the distinction between faith and ideology places the relationship between the Church and the world of liberal culture, politics, and economics in a new light. Through much of modern history, this world seemed an adversary, even a declared enemy, of Christianity and of the Catholic Church in particular. Opposition to the Church— inasmuch as it was a reaction to an ideological Christianity (whose most flagrant outbreak produced the wars of religion)—had serious motivations. Yet in opposing the Church and faith itself, it, too, succumbed to ideology. In the name of freedom, equality, and fraternity, it was capable of sinking in the Seine barges full of nuns handcuffed at the wrists. Or again, in the name of "a free Church in a free state," it did not hesitate to confiscate Church property, close hospitals and schools, and dissolve religious orders.

From the perspective adopted in *Centesimus Annus,* one can easily see that the true adversary liberal democracy confronted after the Enlightenment was faith reduced to the level of ideology. It is also easier to understand that the antagonists of Christianity were not democracy, liberalism, and capitalism but rather their ideological interpretations. Moreover, it is now evident, as it was not for earlier generations, that democracy, liberalism, and modern economics were conceived in a Christian culture and constitute some of its most important expressions.

CULTURE

Let us hasten to add that a vigorous culture is indispensable for the proper functioning of these institutions. They require a culture that, without taking its cues strictly from Christian inspiration, converges with Christian anthropology. The paradox is that, in fact and in principle, liberal political and economic institutions are not able to forge such a culture.

According to Walter Kasper's diagnosis, the secular liberal society is incapable of discovering ultimate justifications for itself, and therefore the values on which it is built erode. Kasper writes, "Society, for the sake of its own survival, is reliant on authorities independent of it that stand for the meaning of freedom and encourage freedom for all. In the past it was sometimes necessary to fight for freedom against a theological or clerical absolutism. Today a new situation has arisen. Religion belongs today to the conditions for the survival of our free culture."[27]

To be more precise, Christianity—for that is indeed what is in question here—is the necessary condition for the survival of liberal culture, even if that sounds simply iconoclastic to both Catholics and leaders of secular culture. Although John Paul never explicitly states such a radical thesis in *Centesimus Annus,* the central thread of the encyclical is the same as Kasper's affirmation. In the pope's description, the core of a vigorous culture resides in the question posed individually and collectively about transcendent truth—that is, in the mystery of God and religion. In a world without truth, freedom loses its meaning and the economy its efficiency, while politics yields to the temptation of totalitarian solutions and the individual and society become alienated. John Paul's rigorous critique of democratic capitalism derives from this diagnosis.

Here a question arises: Is it of the essence of a liberal culture, economy, and politics to eliminate transcendent truth from social life?

The question is posed only implicitly in the encyclical, but the pope provides an explicit response. Having stressed that the truth is constitutive of culture and anthropology, and having taken good note of the market economy, democracy, and the open culture, John Paul affirms that it is possible—and indeed necessary—to build a free society respectful of the value of the Absolute.

Such a line of thinking, though certainly controversial to many contemporary liberals, has some weighty historical arguments on its side. The history of modern Europe can be seen as the transformation of a *verital* society (to borrow Romano Guardini's term) into a liberal society. A verital society (derived from the word *veritas,* or truth) is one whose life is organized according to the transcendent truth its people profess—in the case of Europe, Christian truth. From this perspective, it is easy to detect a "modern dishonesty" inscribed in the very birth of liberalism.[28]

Liberalism opposed the verital order—the Christian society, the Church and the culture it propagated—in the name of freedom and the autonomy of the individual. This opposition, in theory and in practice, had an eminently political, or more broadly social, dimension. Despite its anti-Christian and anti-Catholic character, liberalism was not deliberately a metaphysical revolt. John Hallowell reminds us that the liberal rebellion against the established order had serious motivations and was justified: "The individual of the seventeenth century was . . . hedged in and restrained politically, socially, and economically by arbitrary, personal authority. These restraints not only impeded the expansion and development of free, private economic enterprise but were also incompatible in principle with the basic liberal postulate of the essential moral worth and equality of human personality."[29] But liberalism's concept of a society composed of autonomous, enlightened individuals was built on two pillars: freedom, the guarantor of the autonomy of man, and truth or, more precisely, the infallible discernment of absolute truth by enlightened reason. Proponents of this cause maintained the unshakable conviction that there exists, in John Locke's words, "law, and that too, as intelligible and plain to a rational creature, and a studier of that law, as the positive laws of commonwealths; nay, possibly plainer; as much as reason is easier to be understood, than the fancies and intricate contrivances of men."[30] As Hallowell observes, "to this anarchic conception of society [liberalism] counterposed the belief in the existence of a transcendental order of truth which is accessible to man's natural reason and capable of evoking a moral response."[31]

Enlightenment thinkers were convinced that the anthropological truth Christianity brings, and the moral truth intricately connected with it, are "natural" or "universal" and that perception of the truth is evident and certain. This conviction permitted them—subconsciously at least—to consider these truths their own.[32] The appropriation would bring a cascade of consequences. Guardini sums up his critique of this "modern dishonesty":

> Non-Christian culture commenced its growth at the very outset of the modern age. At first, the attack upon Christianity was directed against the content of Revelation. It was not made against those ethical values, individual or social, which had been perfected under the inspiration of the Faith. At the same time modern culture claimed those very values as its own foundation. Due largely to its changes in historic study, the modern world dedicated itself to the theory that it had discovered and developed ethical values.

It is true, indeed, that the modern age did further the intrinsic worth of personality, of individual freedom, of responsibility and dignity, of man's inherent potentiality for mutual respect and help. These human values began their development, however, during earliest Christian times, while the Middle Ages continued their nurture by its cultivation of the interior and religious life. But the modern era suffered the invasion of consciousness by personal autonomy; human perfection became a cultural acquisition independent of ethics or of Christianity. This point of view was expressed in many ways by many groups, pre-eminently in the voicing of "the Rights of Man" during the French Revolution. In truth, all human values find their root in Revelation.[33]

The naive optimism of the Enlightenment, its belief in reason's infallible ability to discern transcendent truth, the rejection of sin joined to the certitude of "private vices, public benefits," an unconscious appropriation of numerous elements of Christian ethics and anthropology—all these factors aggravated the problem. Enlightenment thinkers managed to recognize as "natural" the benefits the Gospel brought to the world, while presenting Christianity, and notably the Catholic Church, as monuments to deception and hypocrisy.

French scholar Paul Hazard comments that the Enlightenment encyclopedists "made up mock sermons; they invented stories in dubious taste, and more than dubious anecdotes, for a dash of the indecent found a ready place in their armoury." The result, says Hazard, was a Christianity stripped bare "of any trace in history save an injurious one, with not a single problematical good point, not so much as the semblance of a virtue."[34] Such an attitude inevitably widened the chasm separating Catholic thought from European liberal democracy.

Today, as a result of secularization, the cultural contradictions of capitalism, a distressed faith in progress, and a more general doubt about the universality of Western culture and the certitude of rational cognition are more and more in evidence. Christopher Dawson foretold this outcome: "The Liberal faith owed its strength to the elements that it had derived from the religious tradition that it attempted to replace. Thus, in so far as it succeeded in secularizing European culture, it undermined the foundations on which its own existence depended. Instead of uniting Europe in a new spiritual unity, it had helped to destroy the spiritual tradition to which European culture owed its unity and its very existence."[35]

The state and the economic system endeavor to assure a maximum of liberty to the citizens without judging the veracity of their convictions. But a political and economic agnosticism (which is necessary condition for the existence of a democratic capitalist state) led to an anthropological agnosticism, where it is impossible to speak with certainty about the nature of man or to judge his choices, and finally to a metaphysical agnosticism, where there is no absolute truth. The concept of freedom likewise evolved, from the concept of political freedom, where the political structures do not interfere in the manner in which individuals use their individual liberty, through an anthropological conception, where all human choices enjoy parity of rights, to an ideological conception, where social life ought to be organized so as not to favor any human option over another.

Postmodernism, characterized by individualism and radical relativism, was born of the rejection of the Enlightenment heritage.[36] It is not, however, a negation of the Enlightenment mind. Rather it is a consequence of it—of the "modern dishonesty" that appropriates Christian ethics while opposing transcendent principles.[37] What Daniel Bell called "pop hedonism," according to which the main organizing force of Western society is consumption, was virtually contained in it. So, too, was an invasive relativism that results, in its mild form, in a distancing from the truth and, in a harsher version, in an outright hostility to the very concept of truth.[38]

This is the culture that John Paul critiques in *Centesimus Annus,* a culture that is not only deeply non-Christian but also hostile to Christianity. The encyclical makes a new and significant contribution to Church teaching by showing how in such a world, liberal institutions erode, making that culture an enemy not just of Christianity but also of democracy and the liberal economy.

Is Democratic Capitalism Doomed?

Is there any turning back from this process? According to some social scientists, the answer is no—the erosion of liberal democracy has already gone too far to be stopped. Others place their hope in a "revenge of the sacred" that is starting to surface in our culture.[39]

One thing is certain: the expansion of this culture will force liberal democracy to confront questions that until now it has deliberately attempted to elude. These questions touch on doctrines held to be sacred, such as the equality of rights of all minorities and cultures—a view, however generously motivated, that inevitably leads to social atomization. Questions also arise from the more and more invasive globalization of life. For example, the continued promotion of consumer culture is not simply unfavorable to any religious organization; it also exacerbates anti-Western reaction.[40]

Beyond that, by revealing the lack of a worldwide consensus on the principles of social life, globalization ends up unmasking the naive Enlightenment faith in the natural and universal character of the truths discovered by reason. As Samuel Huntington wrote, "At a superficial level much of Western culture has indeed permeated the rest of the world. At a more basic level, however, Western concepts differ fundamentally from those prevalent in other civilizations. Western ideas of individualism, liberalism, constitutionalism, human rights, equality, liberty, the rule of law, democracy, free markets, the separation of church and state, often have little resonance in Islamic, Confucian, Japanese, Hindu, Buddhist, or Orthodox cultures. Western efforts to propagate such ideas produce instead a reaction against 'human rights imperialism' and a reaffirmation of indigenous values, as can be seen in the support for religious fundamentalism by the younger generation in non-Western cultures."[41]

Confrontation between cultures is inescapable. This dynamic poses a new challenge to Western civilization,

which is founded on the dignity of the person, the importance of social bonds, and a common view of the objectives
of social life. Will that foundation endure?

THE CHURCH, SAVIOR OF LIBERALISM?

It remains to be seen whether the element in liberal culture that can destroy democratic capitalism is a secondary problem in the eyes of the Church. Historian Arnold
Toynbee argued that if liberal institutions collapsed,
Christianity would not collapse alongside them: "If our
secular Western civilization perishes, Christianity may be
expected not only to endure but to grow in wisdom and
stature as the result of a fresh experience of secular catas-
trophe."[42] Clearly, though, the fate of liberal institutions is
a crucial concern for defenders of democratic capitalism.

The diagnosis in *Centesimus Annus* is far from pessimistic. John Paul recognizes what is at stake in the decline
of Western civilization, which he calls "the great site of
education and culture," and he shows what is needed to
sustain it. To survive and flourish, the market economy
and democratic politics must recognize the fundamental
importance of transcendent truth and create a vigorous
cultural system capable of preserving an "anthropological
minimum," that common vision of dignity of man shared
by people of different religions and worldviews.

Why has the transition from a verital to a liberal
society taken the form of conflict? Effectively, liberalism
drove back the verital society in the name of freedom,
appropriating the achievements of the verital order and

fashioning a culture and institutions that marginalize or flatly eliminate the original sources of cultural and institutional vitality. Where the Christian culture gave shape to freedom by associating it with responsibility, the Enlightenment culture produced an ideology of liberty according to which freedom is justified by itself. Any mention of responsibility for actions, the morality of choices, or the consequences of deeds is seen as an attack on freedom.

At the end of *Centesimus Annus*, John Paul foresees that "in a world without truth, freedom loses its foundation."[43] Meanwhile, Zygmunt Bauman, who writes frequently about postmodernity, consumerism, and globalization, asserts that the sole universal trait in today's world is motion—except this is Brownian motion, or chaos. They are, in effect, saying the same thing, only in different languages.

The challenge is to know whether a society is viable if it is composed of atomized individuals moving and colliding chaotically. More to the point, can a society so constituted survive when it adopts democratic capitalism as its system of political-economic organization? *Centesimus Annus* offers an unambiguous response: *No*. The internal conditions will tear it asunder.

Liberalism has actually performed a service to the Church by forcing her to confront the challenge of freedom. Modern developments in the liberal order have enabled the Church to perceive the problem underlying the distortion of the truth into ideology and the dangers of reducing faith to ideology. *Centesimus Annus* provides ample proof of a truth stripped of ideology. But the encyclical goes further, demonstrating that freedom and truth support each other, and that rupturing their bond will destroy them both.

If this diagnosis is correct, it leads to one last question: Is liberal culture ready to purify freedom of all ideology? The question so far has not been answered, except that under the pontificate of John Paul II—who privileged respect for freedom as a pedagogy—the Church presented herself as one of the few partners of liberal culture that could reinforce this work of ideological purging. Thus it seems that the Church, for so long seen as liberalism's adversary, is positioned to be its savior—but only if the liberal culture is willing to accept the proffered aid.

POPE FRANCIS AND THE
CRISIS OF THE MODERN ECONOMY

My main goal in writing this book was to describe papal teachings concerning democratic capitalism. I focused on reconstructing the popes' attitudes toward free-market economies without constraining myself strictly to economic issues, since political systems and the broader culture heavily influence economics.

In reviewing the *magisterium pontificium* from the late nineteenth century to the present, we can identify two broad categories of papal thinking on economics. Both approaches look at the condition of the contemporary world in the light of the Gospel, but they differ in the scope of their analysis and pronouncements. The first school of thought is characterized by a holistic approach to economic and social issues and a realism in its suggested solutions; the second is characterized by a more selective approach to problems and a focus on decrying injustices in social life rather than showing how to prevent such injustices.

The first method—the "holistic" school, we might call it—tries to offer a realistic depiction of the social situation in which problems have arisen. It also tries to diagnose causes and suggest ways to eliminate pathologies. It appeals mainly (but implicitly) to decision makers in economic and political life.

The second approach—the "pastoral" school—focuses on exposing those situations that need redress. Being more emotional in character, it appeals primarily to public opinion. This approach clearly identifies injustice in the world, but it does not point the way toward realistic remedies. As a result, the pastoral approach can suffer from moralization and a lack of coherence.

Both approaches have been present in Christian reflection from the very beginning. In ancient times, Clement of Alexandria represented the first school of thought, while John Chrysostom represented the second. In the Middle Ages, Thomas Aquinas took the first approach; Bernard of Clairvaux took the second. Later, Antoninus of Florence represented the first option; another famous citizen of that city, Girolamo Savonarola, represented the second.

Among popes, too, the two approaches have been evident. For example, Leo XIII and Pius XI represented the holistic school, whereas Paul VI and Benedict XVI took the pastoral approach. Looking back over Catholic social thought since the late nineteenth century, we can observe that papal teachings on economics have exhibited shifts in emphasis over time. As Table 1 demonstrates, the holistic approach was evident in the first several decades—with

TABLE 1: THE EVOLUTION OF CATHOLIC SOCIAL THOUGHT

	Private property	Free market	Limited state intervention	Socialism	Central planning	Democracy	"Third way"
Rerum Novarum (1891)	positive	positive	positive	negative	neutral	neutral	positive
Quadragesimo Anno (1931)	positive	positive/negative	positive	negative	negative	neutral	positive
Pius XII (1939–1958)	positive	positive	positive	negative	negative	positive	positive
Mater et Magistra (1961)	positive	neutral	positive	neutral	neutral	positive	N/A
Pacem in Terris (1963)	N/A	neutral	positive	N/A	N/A	positive	N/A
Gaudium et Spes (1965)	N/A	neutral	N/A	neutral	neutral	N/A	N/A
Populorum Progressio (1967)	neutral	N/A	N/A	neutral	positive	neutral	positive
Octogesima Adveniens (1971)	neutral	neutral	neutral	positive	positive	neutral	positive
Laborem Exercens (1981)	N/A	neutral	neutral	N/A	negative	neutral	positive
Sollicitudo Rei Socialis (1987)	neutral	N/A	positive/negative	N/A	negative	positive	negative
Centesimus Annus (1991)	positive	positive	positive	negative	negative	positive	negative
Caritas in Veritate (2009)	neutral	positive/negative	positive	neutral	positive	N/A	N/A

= positive estimation   = negative estimation   = neutral   N/A = topic only touched on

Leo XIII's encyclical *Rerum Novarum* (1891), Pius XI's *Quadragesimo Anno* (1931), and the teachings of Pius XII in the 1940s and '50s (contained in addresses and encyclicals that do not focus specifically on social issues). The shift toward the pastoral approach began with John XXIII's *Mater et Magistra* (1961) and accelerated with his *Pacem in Terris* (1963) and then the Second Vatican Council's *Gaudium et Spes* (1965). Only with the papacy of John Paul II did this trend begin to reverse. In fact, John Paul's encyclicals—from *Laborem Exercens* (1981), to *Sollicitudo Rei Socialis* (1987), to *Centesimus Annus* (1991)—reveal a clear evolution from the pastoral approach to the holistic school, as his teachings synthesize the various elements of social life. Eighteen years after *Centesimus Annus*, in *Caritas in Veritate* (2009), Benedict XVI signaled a turn back to the pastoral approach.

How to account for these shifts? It appears that the holistic encyclicals were written during periods when popes were aware that their solutions might be adopted in certain countries. This is true in the cases of Leo XIII (the Church's first statement on modern industrial capitalism, which had an especially significant influence in Catholic-majority countries), Pius XI (in the midst of the Great Depression), and John Paul II (particularly influential in the former Eastern Bloc nations after the collapse of communism). When the responsibility for influencing the shape of social life was lesser, popes took on the role of commentators who critically addressed the abuses evident in social life. Not being tied up in current political trends allowed popes to embrace the principle of "eschatological reservation," to use a term popularized by the Catholic theologian Johann Baptist Metz. This principle, which recognizes that human actions are always (and necessarily) incomplete and temporary, invites critical engagement with the world around us, especially its social and political problems, as a way to identify our present inadequacies.

But by being more selective in their approach and tailored narrowly to the present, "pastoral" critical assessments have been more susceptible to the "spirit of the age." The influence of the zeitgeist is pronounced in papal documents of the 1960s and becomes even clearer in Paul VI's apostolic letter *Octogesima Adveniens*, written in 1971. Paul's letter describes the appeal of socialism to Catholics and suggests that socialism and Catholicism are not opposed. *Octogesima Adveniens* and the encyclicals *Pacem in Terris* and *Populorum Progressio* (1967) are marked so profoundly by the spirit of the times in which they were written that they have much less to say to our situation today than do *Rerum Novarum* and *Quadragesimo Anno*, holistic encyclicals written decades earlier.

This is why *Centesimus Annus*, richer in the lessons of the twentieth century and at the same time referring back to the holistic tradition, can be received as a creative contribution to the debate on the shape of culture, politics, and economics in the twenty-first century.

WHAT ABOUT POPE FRANCIS?

Any reader of this book will naturally wonder how Pope Francis fits into the long tradition of Catholic social teaching on economics. Since Francis was elevated to the papacy in March 2013, Catholics and non-Catholics alike have carefully examined his formal statements and public remarks to determine the direction in which he is leading the Church.

Unfortunately, much of the commentary on Pope Francis has missed the mark. In the introduction to this book I quoted Samuel Gregg on "the limits of applying secular political categories to something like the Catholic Church." Too often the analysis of Pope Francis's statements reveal these limits. Misconceptions abound.

When it comes to economics and political systems, the first misconception is that we can definitively characterize Pope Francis's social teaching. The truth is that Francis's teaching cannot yet be classified, because as of this writing he has not developed it in the form of an encyclical. This book focuses on social encyclicals for a reason: they provide the most fully developed—and authoritative—pronouncements on the Church's social teaching.

In November 2013 Pope Francis did release an apostolic exhortation—less authoritative than an encyclical—entitled *Evangelii Gaudium* (The Joy of the Gospel). Among the exhortation's approximately three hundred paragraphs, only eight refer explicitly to the contemporary economy. Those eight paragraphs drew much attention from American commentators. The conservative talk radio host Rush Limbaugh went so far as to call *Evangelii Gaudium* "pure Marxism." At the other end of the political spectrum, the left-wing magazine *The Nation* declared that Francis had delivered "a direct reproof to capitalism."[1]

But rather than trying to force the pope's pronouncements into secular political categories, we must understand what Francis is saying in *Evangelii Gaudium*—and what he is not.

First, *Evangelii Gaudium* is not about economics per se; it is about the Catholic Church's mission of evangelization and the joy of preaching the Gospel, and at the same time about the challenges the Church faces in the contemporary world.

Also, the eight paragraphs that deal with economics contain neither an analysis of economic mechanisms nor a recommendation for concrete reforms. Rather, Pope Francis critiques dangerous aspects of modern culture. He almost shouts in his exhortation: *No* to a "throwaway" culture! *No* to "a globalization of indifference"! *No* to the "idolatry of money"!

Many commentators have tried to read into such statements a new development in Church teaching: a condemnation of the market economy. That is what Rush Limbaugh and *The Nation* did. But for all the forceful language, Pope Francis does in *Evangelii Gaudium* what many popes before him have done: he shows the dangers that arise when the market (or the state) is elevated to an absolute in itself—when man's spiritual dimensions are subordinated to his material ones.

Francis stressed this continuity with Catholic social teaching after *Evangelii Gaudium* prompted an outcry from some conservatives. In an interview with an Italian newspaper, the pope declared flatly, "Marxist ideology is wrong." He added, "There is nothing in the exhortation that cannot be found in the social doctrine of the church."[2]

Pope Francis is correct. Recall that in *Centesimus Annus*, John Paul II warns about the risk of "idolatry" of the market, about the dangers that come when economic life is "absolutized." When Francis writes of the crisis that arises from "the denial of the primacy of the human person," he echoes John Paul's statement that when economic freedom becomes the *only* freedom, it "loses its necessary relationship to the human person."[3]

All that said, the forceful tone of Francis's exhortation cannot be ignored. As one commentator put it, "The statements of Pope Francis have certainly been more spirited than we have heard for a while—complete with exclamation marks, extremely rare in papal documents."[4] In Francis's early statements we can quite clearly see a "pastoral" sensitivity. This pope, in his way of talking about social reality, fits much better in the tradition represented by Paul VI's *Populorum Progressio* and Benedict XVI's *Caritas in Veritate* than in that of Leo XIII's *Rerum Novarum* and John Paul II's *Centesimus Annus*.

Confronting the "Enlightenment Paradigm"

I had a second reason for writing *Papal Economics*: I recognized in Catholic social teaching the necessary counterweight to a particularly narrow and, I daresay, ideological approach to economic issues, one that has dominated the past few centuries.

The birth of modern economics is generally traced to 1776, the year that marked the publication of Adam Smith's famous *Inquiry into the Nature and Causes of the Wealth of Nations*. We should actually look back almost a century earlier, to 1687. That is when Isaac Newton published his most celebrated opus, *Philosophiæ Naturalis Principia Mathematica*.

Newton's work said nothing about economics, of course. But in laying out the law of universal gravitation and the laws of motion, Newton strongly influenced Enlightenment thinkers. This influence had little to do with mathematical problems: Voltaire, who devoted a book to Newton's work, simply did not understand them. Rather, with his discoveries, Newton restored man's central position in the universe, which Copernicus had undermined. For it turned out that the human mind was capable of discovering the universe's laws and invisible forces, and therefore of unraveling its mysteries. Here was the source of the next century's fast-spreading conviction of the omnipotence of human reason. The religion of progress was born, and it soon conquered Western culture. Chemists, psychologists, economists, historians, biologists, sociologists (the father of sociology, August Comte, spoke mostly of *physique sociale*, or "social physics")—all these and more embraced the idea of the human mind's unlimited capabilities.

And just as Newton identified an invisible force that governed bodies, Enlightenment thinkers welcomed the idea of an unseen force that ruled the individual human psyche and social and economic life. Thus the *invisible hand*—a term Adam Smith used only three times, in three different meanings and in three different works (once in his *History of Astronomy!*)—became a "philosopher's stone" of mainstream Western economic thought. Much like the universal gravitational force in physics, the *invisible hand* in economics emerged as the unseen but undeniable force that explains everything and governs absolutely.

The idea of the *invisible hand* followed naturally from an idea, unknown to Smith, that economic life is amoral. Bernard Mandeville presented the latter concept in his *Fable of the Bees* (1714), which is best summarized by its subtitle, *Private Vices, Public Benefits*: it turns out that the "private vices" of self-interest and indulging human desires lead to the "public benefit" of increased wealth. The eighteenth-century French physiocrat Vincent de Gournay captured the idea of the *invisible hand* with his maxim *"Laissez faire et laissez passer, le monde va de lui même!"* (Let do and let pass, the world goes on by itself!).

This pervasive mind-set, strengthened by the advances of the Industrial Revolution, led economists to try to put their profession on par with the hard sciences, capable of being reduced to "objective," "iron" laws and mathematical formulas. As a result, economics was depersonalized and leeched of an ethical dimension. In the nineteenth and twentieth centuries, astute critics including Ordoliberals and economists of the Austrian School recognized the dangerous and inhumane assumptions underlying modern economics, but their criticisms could not penetrate to the mainstream. That is because incredible economic growth over the long term veiled the existence of structural problems.

Today, however, the consequences of eroding the cultural foundations of Western societies—that is, the foundations of Christian anthropology and Christian ethics—cannot be ignored. As economic growth stagnates worldwide and the economists' mathematical models grow more complex but display less predictive power, the chorus of doubt about the "Enlightenment paradigm" grows louder. That dogmatic way of understanding economic life seems more and more unfit for today's reality. No longer can we openly praise the rejection of ethical standards ("Greed is good"). We are witnessing a growing appreciation for the importance of ethical foundations, particularly as the source of interpersonal trust, which enables the cooperation essential to a market economy. It is no surprise, therefore, that books saying things quite obvious from the point of view of Catholic social teaching—such as Michael Sandel's *What Money Can't Buy: The Moral Limits of Markets* and Tomas Sedlacek's *Economics of Good and Evil*—have attracted wide readerships. Nor is it a surprise that a reflection on economic inequality like Thomas Piketty's *Capital in the Twenty-First Century* has become an international sensation.

All these developments informed my desire to write *Papal Economics.* I have attempted to show that the social thought of the Catholic Church represents a creative alternative to the Enlightenment paradigm that has dominated economic thought for centuries. The personalistic perspective of Catholic social thought, I believe, finds its fullest and most coherent expression in John Paul II's *Centesimus Annus.* John Paul's teaching also represented a counterweight to the twentieth century's statism (a belief in an omnipotent state) and constructivism (a belief that a new man could be created), two other ideas spawned by Enlightenment thinking. Those ideas manifested themselves in centralized, even totalitarian states and centrally planned economies. Then the collapse of "real socialism" offered definitive proof of the ineffectiveness of statist solutions. That was not the end of the matter, however. More recent crises in the Western world—the bursting of the dot-com bubble (2001), the worldwide collapse in financial and banking markets (2007–8), the crisis in the eurozone (2010)—have increased doubts about an Enlightenment paradigm that sees man as *homo economicus.*

Thus we have reason to hope that in this century the paradigm of "purely scientific" economics (reductive and depersonalized) will be replaced with a more "human" economy. In this matter Catholic social thought can be an important partner in the public debate. This is what I wanted to show in *Papal Economics.*

Last but certainly not least: I would like *de profundis et ex toto corde meo* to thank Michael Novak, Mark Henrie, Jed Donahue, Thomas Posatko, and Matthew Gerken—without their great kindness, competence, and engagement, this book would not have appeared.

Maciej Zięba, OP
August 2014

NOTES

INTRODUCTION: CAPITALISM, FREEDOM, AND TRUTH

1. Samuel Gregg, "Pope Francis: A Man of the Left?," *Acton Commentary*, March 20, 2013, www.acton.org/pub/commentary/2013/03/20/pope-francis-man-left.

CHAPTER 1: A BRIEF HISTORY OF DEMOCRATIC CAPITALISM IN CATHOLIC SOCIAL TEACHING

1. Oswald von Nell-Breuning, *Reorganization of Social Economy: The Social Encyclical Developed and Explained* (New York: Bruce Publishing Company, 1936), 136. Nell-Breuning was referring here to Leo's statement that "it may be truly said that it is only by the labor of working men that States grow rich." Leo uses the Latin phrase *divitias civitatum*, which means "wealth of nations." See Michael Novak, *Catholic Social Thought and Liberal Institutions: Freedom with Justice*, 2nd ed. (New Brunswick, NJ: Transaction, 1989), 86.
2. *Rerum Novarum*, 34, 18, 4, 18. (Numbers refer to paragraphs in

English translations of all cited papal encyclicals, which can be found on Vatican website: www.vatican.va.)

3. In another of his encyclicals, Leo writes that "the civil power . . . was established for the common good" (*Immortale Dei, 5*).

4. William Murphy, "*Rerum Novarum*," in *A Century of Catholic Social Thought*, ed. George Weigel and Robert Royal (Washington, DC: Ethics and Public Policy Center, 1991), 17.

5. Johannes Schasching, "*Die geistigen Hintergründe und die aktuellen sozialen Probleme von Rerum novarum*," in *Colloquium salutis* 1982, nos. 14, 18.

6. *Rerum Novarum*, 14.

7. Ibid., 36.

8. See Franz H. Mueller, *The Church and the Social Question* (Washington, DC: AEI, 1984), 79–81; Patrick de Laubier, *La pensée sociale de l'Église catholique, un idéal historique de Léon XIII à Jean-Paul II* (Fribourg: Éd universitaires, 1984).

9. See Pius XI, *Quadragesimo Anno* (1931), no. 79. On the subsidiarity principle, see George Weigel, *Soul of the World: Notes on the Future of Public Catholicism* (Washington, DC, 1996, 109); Peter L. Berger and Richard John Neuhaus, *To Empower People: The Role of Mediating Structures and Public Policy* (Washington, DC, 1997), 157–201.

10. *Rerum Novarum*, 27, 12.

11. Ibid., 55, 56.

12. Mueller, *The Church and the Social Question*, 78–79.

13. *Rerum Novarum*, 27, 49.

14. Ibid., 49.

15. Mueller, *The Church and the Social Question*, 82.

16. Murphy, "*Rerum Novarum*," 13–14.

17. Cardinal Joseph Höffner, *Christliche Gesellschaftslehre* (Kevelaer: Butzon & Bercker, 1983), chap. 2.

18. De Laubier, *La pensée sociale*, 43.

19. Murphy, "*Rerum Novarum*," 23.

20. In the years 1931–32, more than five thousand banks went bankrupt in the United States, and in 1933, almost four hundred.

21. For example, on Thursday, October 24, 1929, eleven Wall Street businessmen committed suicide.

22. The gross national product in the United States fell from 104.6 in 1929 to 56.1 in 1933, while world production in 1933 amounted to 67 percent of the 1928 level. In England, France, Germany, and Italy, exports and imports decreased 60–70 percent in comparison with 1921.

23. In the United States, the unemployment rate increased from 3.2 percent in 1929 to 24.9 in 1933. In France, industrial employment fell 18 percent in comparison to 1928; in Germany, it fell 41 percent.

24. *Quadragesimo Anno*, 109, 108.

25. Ibid., 10.

26. Ibid., 14.

27. Ibid., 10, 44, 112, 116.

28. Ibid., 118, 119, 120.

29. See Rodger Charles, SJ, and Drostan Maclaren, OP, *The Social Teaching of Vatican II* (Oxford: Plater Publications, 1982), 324: "Since the type supported by the encyclical was one based on free association and stressed the value of such organizations in relieving the state of many of its burdens, the Italian/Fascist type of corporatism, which was both imposed from above and denied the right of association in free trade unions, far from being recommended was in fact being condemned."

30. *Quadragesimo Anno*, 126, 57, 88. De Laubier comments: "Social charity, which should not be confused with the charitable aid dispensed as help to which everyone is obliged in conscience, can be compared to that friendship which Aristotle situates at the center of his political theory and which he considers as indispensable for the proper functioning of the state" (*De Laubier, La pensée sociale*, 77).

31. Wilhelm Röpke, "Liberalism and Christianity," in *Modern Age: The First Twenty-Five Years, A Selection*, ed. George A. Panichas (Indianapolis: Liberty Press, 1988), 516.

32. *Quadragesimo Anno*, 101, 112.

33. Ibid., 51, 74.

34. Ibid., 47.

35. Ibid., 49, 78.

36. Ibid., 79.

37. Novak, *Catholic Social Thought*, 111.

38. Röpke, "Liberalism and Christianity," 515–16.

39. Czeslaw Strzeszewski, *Ewolucja Katolickiej Nauki Spolecznej* (Warsaw: O rodek Dokumentacji i Studiów Społecznych, 1978), 195.

40. Novak, *Catholic Social Thought*, 128.

41. *Mater et Magistra*, 51, 53, 55.

42. Ibid., 57, 58.

43. Ibid., 114, 115.

44. Ibid., 105–7.

45. Novak, *Catholic Social Thought*, 127.

46. *Mater et Magistra*, 219. Novak uses a different English translation of *Mater et Magistra* from the one used elsewhere in this book.

47. Novak, *Catholic Social Thought*, 130.

48. *Mater et Magistra*, 59–87,

49. Marc Jussieu, "*Mater et Magistra*," *Esprit*, (June 1962), 940.

50. *Mater et Magistra*, 34.

51. Ibid., 160.

52. Ibid., 132.

53. Jussieu, "*Mater et Magistra*," 942.

54. Cardinal Léon Joseph Suenens, in his discourse delivered March 13, 1963, on the occasion of *Pacem in Terris*, at the seat of the United Nations in New York.

55. *Pacem in Terris*, 121, 122, 123.

56. Ibid., 67, 120.

57. Ibid., 52, 68, 79.

58. Ibid., 158, 159, 161, 162.

59. Anglo-Saxon commentators, especially, have observed that John XXIII presented many useful reflections in this encyclical, but completely failed to propose any means of their realization. See, for instance, John Courtney Murray, "Things Old and New in *Pacem in Terris*," *America*, April 27, 1973; Reinhold Niebuhr, "*Pacem in Terris*: Two Views," *Christianity and Crisis*, May 13, 1968; Paul Ramsay, "*Pacem in Terris*" in *The Just War: Force and Political Responsibility* (New York: Rowman and Littlefield, 1968).

60. See Paul VI, *Le developpement des peuples—Populorum progressio. Introduction de Vincent Cosmao* (Paris: Centurion, 1967);

Georges Jarlot, "Lo sviluppo economico e la pace nel mondo nel' enciclica *Populorum progressio*," *La Civiltá Cattolica*, June 1, 1967); L. Bagliolo, *La Pace e Paolo VI* (Rome: Pontificia Universita Lateranense, 1969); D. Alberti, *L'umanesimo plenario della 'Populorum progressio'* (Rome: Pontificia Universita Lateranense, 1972); de Laubier, *La pensée sociale*.

61. See, for example, Milton Friedman, "Papal Economics," Newsweek, April 24, 1967; Peter T. Bauer, "Ecclesiastical Economics Is Envy Exalted," *This World* 1 (Winter/Spring 1982); Robert Royal, "*Populorum Progressio*," in Weigel and Royal, *A Century of Catholic Social Thought*; Novak, *Catholic Social Thought*.

62. Strzeszewski, *Ewolucja Katolickiej Nauki Spolecznej*, 173.

63. L. Gruppi, "Der italienische Weg zum Sozialismus," in *Schopfertum und Freiheit in einer humanen Gesellschaft* (Vienna: Europa Verlag, 1969), 298.

64. *Populorum Progressio*, 25, 26.

65. Novak, *Catholic Social Thought*, 135.

66. *Populorum Progressio*, 61.

67. Ibid., 57.

68. The greatest producers of wheat, feed, coal, wood, and cotton were, at that time, the United States and Canada. (See John Kenneth Galbraith, "The Defense of the Multinational Company," *Harvard Business Review*, March/April 1978.) On the other hand, what wealthy countries import from developing nations includes cloth, shoes, and electronic goods.

69. *Populorum Progressio*, 30–31.

70. Oliver F. Williams, "Introduction" to *Co-Creation and Capitalism— John Paul II's 'Laborem Exercens,'* ed. I. B. Houck and Oliver F. Williams (Washington, DC: University Press of America, 1983), 2.

71. Michael Novak, "Creation Theology," in Houck and Williams, *Co-Creation and Capitalism*, 18.

72. Nicholas von Hoffman, "The Anti-Monetarist Pope," *Spectator*, October 10, 1981, 11.

73. Peter F. Lawler, ed., *Papal Economies* (Washington, DC: Heritage Foundation, 1982).

74. *Laborem Exercens*, 14.

75. Ibid.

76. Ibid., 7.

77. Houck and Williams, *Co-Creation and Capitalism*, 24.

78. *Laborem Exercens*, 13.

79. Ibid., 17.

80. Ibid., 15, 18.

81. Ibid., 14.

82. Ibid., 14.

83. Ibid., 18.

84. See, for instance, Novak, *Catholic Social Thought*, 149–64; Houck and Williams, *Co-Creation and Capitalism*, 17–41.

85. *Sollicitudo Rei Socialis*, 21.

86. Ibid., 48.

87. Ibid., 41.

88. Such a view has been criticized, especially in the United States. See, for instance, Peter Berger, "Empirical Testing," in *Aspiring to Freedom*, ed. Kenneth A. Myers (Grand Rapids, MI: Eerdmans, 1988); William F. Buckley Jr., "What Is the Pope Saying?" *National Review*, March 18, 1988; William McGurn, "*Sollicitudo rei socialis*," in Weigel and Royal, *A Century of Catholic Social Thought*, 101; William Safire, "Structures of Sin," *New York Times*, February 22, 1988.

89. *Sollicitudo Rei Socialis*, 37, 36.

90. Ibid., 44.

91. Ibid., 15.

92. Ibid., 28.

93. Ibid., 13, 44.

94. Ibid., 42.

95. Ibid., 15, 30.

96. Novak, *Catholic Social Thought*, 243–44.

97. *Pacem in Terris*, 47.

98. *Sollicitudo Rei Socialis*, 42.

99. Royal and Weigel, *A Century of Catholic Social Thought*, 115.

CHAPTER 2: POLITICAL COMMUNITY

1. George Weigel, *The Final Revolution: The Resistance Church and the Collapse of Communism* (New York: Oxford University Press, 1992); Samuel P. Huntington, *The Third Wave: Democratization in the Late Twentieth Century* (Norman: University of Oklahoma Press, 1993).

2. This aspect of the encyclical was analyzed by, among others, L. Roos, "*Centesimus annus*, ein Meilenstein in Sozialverkündingung der Kirche," *BKU Ausgewählte Vorträge* no. 15 (1991); "A Report and Commentary on the Peace, Freedom, and Security Debate from the Ethics and Public Policy Center," vol. 5, no. 5 (May–June 1991): "The New, New Things—Pope John Paul II on Human Freedom"; Paul Likoudis, "Pope's New Encyclical Offers Key for World Development in Third Millennium," *The Wanderer* (July 4, 1991).

3. *Centesimus Annus*, 46, 43.

4. See St. Augustine: "As for this mortal life, which ends after a few days' course, what does it matter under whose rule a man lives, being so soon to die, provided that the rulers do not force him to impious and wicked acts?" (St. Augustine, *De civitate Dei*, V, 17); or the teachings of the Second Vatican Council: "The Church, by reason of her role and competence, is not identified with any political community nor bound by ties to any political system" (*Gaudium et Spes*, 76).

5. *Centesimus Annus*, 25.

6. K. Tarnowski, "Poza utopia," *Znak* (no. 6, 1991), 43.

7. See Friedrich A. Hayek, *New Studies in Philosophy, Politics, Economics, and the History of Ideas* (London: Routledge & Kegan Paul, 1978); Friedrich A. Hayek, *Law, Legislation, and Liberty* (Chicago: University of Chicago Press, 1983); Isaiah Berlin, *Two Concepts of Liberty* (Oxford: Clarendon Press, 1958); Milton and Rose Friedman, *Free to Choose: A Personal Statement* (New York: Harcourt, 1990); Karl R. Popper, *The Open Society and Its Enemies*, 2 vols., 5th ed. rev. (London: Routledge & Kegan Paul, 1966); Karl R. Popper, *The Poverty of Historicism* (London: Routledge & Kegan Paul, 1957).

8. *Centesimus Annus*, 46.

9. Ideology, as John Paul II understands it, is not an epistemological concept (as it was for those who coined it, a group of representatives of the French Enlightenment), nor any psychological phenomenon (Freud), but rather belongs to the sphere of social life (as, in Mannheim and Parsons, a sociological phenomenon). It is a worldview with a transcendental justification, accompanied by a concrete plan for the organization of social life. The certainty derived from the possession of an absolute justification and its concrete translation into the level of political practice permits the realization of these solutions by the use of force. Daniel Bell defines ideology in a manner very similar to Pope John Paul II in the article, "Ideology and Soviet Politics," *Slavic Review*, no. 12 (1965), 591–603; Daniel Bell, *The End of Ideology* (New York, 1960). On the definition and history of the concept, see M. Rejai, "Ideology" in *Dictionary of the History of Ideas*, ed. P. P. Wiener (New York, 1973), 553–59.

10. This is one of the fundamental traits that distinguish the Church from an ideological party. As Cardinal Ratzinger (the future Pope Benedict XVI) noticed: "The difference between the structure of a party constituted on ideological grounds and the Church lies precisely in the question of truth." After having underlined that, in ideological parties, truth is absorbed by what the party establishes, Cardinal Ratzinger points out the difference: "The fundamental conviction of Christian faith on the contrary is that at the beginning we have reason and with it truth; it brings forth man and human reason as capable of truth. . . . The community of the Church is admittedly necessary as the historical condition for the activity of reason, but the Church does not coincide with the truth. It is not the constructor of truth but is constructed by it and is the place where it is perceived. Truth therefore remains essentially independent of the Church and the Church is ordered towards it as a means" (Cardinal Joseph Ratzinger, *Church, Ecumenism, and Politics* [New York, Crossroad, 1988], 159–60).

11. Hans Urs von Balthasar, *The von Balthasar Reader*, ed. Medard Kehl and Werner Löser, trans. Robert J. Daly and Fred Lawrence (Edinburgh, 1985), 186.

12. St. Augustine, *De Trinitate*, IV, 24.

13. Ibid., IX, I.

14. One of the most important tasks of the Church is defense of this truth—revealed to us by God and not fully comprehended by our reason—from ideologization. Such is, for instance, the purpose of dogma in theology: "This more powerful incomprehensibility of the biblical God only remains in effect so long as the dogmatic formulae protect it against renewed attempts at rationalization" (von Balthasar, *The von Balthasar Reader*, 276). The Second Vatican Council taught that it is the duty of the church to continually examine and consider divine truth, all the time knowing that never in history—as long as there is space and time—will the Church achieve complete cognizance of it: "As the centuries go by, the Church is always advancing towards the plenitude of divine truth, until eventually the words of God are fulfilled in her" (*Dei Verbum*, 8).

15. Walter Kasper, *The God of Jesus Christ* (New York, 1991), 114–115.

16. *Dignitatis Humanae*, 1, 2.

17. Ratzinger, 162–63. Ratzinger continues: "With this the fundamental task of the Church's political stance, as I understand it, has been defined; its aim must be to maintain this balance of a dual system as the foundation of freedom. Hence the Church must make claims and demands on public law and cannot simply retreat into the private sphere. Hence it must also take care on the other hand that Church and state remain separated and that belonging to the Church clearly retains its voluntary character."

18. *Centesimus Annus*, 8, 39.

19. See Jacques Maritain, *Man and the State* (Chicago, 1951): "Yet if we are to avoid serious misunderstandings, we have to distinguish clearly the State and the Body Politic. These do not belong to diverse categories, but they differ from each another as a part differs from the whole. *The Body Politic* or *the Political Society* is the whole. The State is a part—the topmost part—of this whole" (9–10); "The State is only that part of the body politic especially concerned with the maintenance of law, the promotion of the common welfare and public order, and the administration of public affairs. The State is a part which *specializes* in the interests of the

whole" (12); "The part as such is inferior to the *whole*. The State is inferior to the body politic as a whole, and is at the service of the body politic as a whole" (13).

20. Juan-Miguel M. Garrigues, *L'Église, la société libre et le communisme* (Paris, 1984), 41.

21. *Centesimus Annus*, 49.

22. Pierre Manent, *An Intellectual History of Liberalism*, trans. Rebecca Balinski (Princeton, 1995), 65–66; Juan-Miguel Garrigues also observes, "Liberal states are on the contrary the heirs of all intermediary social communities whose liberties and legitimate autonomies they recognized and guarded" (p. 32).

23. See John Rawls, *Political Liberalism* (New York, 1996), and Ronald Dworkin, *A Matter of Principle* (Cambridge, MA, 1985).

24. *Centesimus Annus*, 41.

25. Ibid., 41.

26. Ibid., 34. Rocco Buttiglione clarifies that this primarily concerns the instinctive needs of man. Respect for liberty, a condition of the realization of the good, is, in Buttiglione's opinion, the ethical justification of the free market. See Rocco Buttiglione, *Il problema politico dei cattolici. Dottrina sociale e modernita* (Cassale Monferrato, 1993), 145.

27. *Centesimus Annus*, 11.

28. Buttiglione, 130.

29. *Centesimus Annus*, 41.

30. Ibid., 14.

31. Ibid., 41, 25.

32. Ibid., 49, 50.

33. Russell Hittinger, "The Pope and the Liberal State," *First Things*, no. 12 (December 1992): 40.

34. *Centesimus Annus*, 48.

35. Let us note a convergence with the position of certain liberal thinkers, such as John Gray, who writes, "The government has the duty to extract members of the poorest and lowest classes from a state of dependency on the state and facilitate their full participation in the civic society." See John Gray, *O rzadzie ograniczonym* (Warszawa, 1995), 20.

36. Buttiglione, 147.

37. *Centesimus Annus*, 48.

38. Richard John Neuhaus, *Doing Well and Doing Good: The Challenge to the Christian Capitalist* (New York, 1992), 242. On the distinction between the body politic and the state in the context of a substantialization and absolutization of the role of the latter, see Maritain, 12–19.

39. Regarding the socially negative effects of the functioning of the welfare state, see Edgar K. Browning, "Income, Distribution, and Redistribution," in *Modern Capitalism* (London, 1987), 84–107; Bertrand de Jouvenel, *The Ethics of Redistribution* (Indianapolis, 1990); D. E. Green, *The Welfare State: For Rich or for Poor* (Washington, DC, 1982); D. E. Green, Equalizing People (London, 1990); R. Harris, A. Seldon, *Welfare without State* (London, 1987); *The Remedy for Poverty* (Grand Rapids, 1996); Gertrude Himmelfarb, "A De-Moralized Society," *Public Interest* (Fall 1994).

40. *Centesimus Annus*, 48, 15.

41. Ibid., 11, 15.

42. This would be a society directed by the subsidiarity principle, of which George Weigel writes, "Negatively, the principle means that the community must not deprive individuals, nor larger communities deprive smaller communities, of the opportunity to do what they can for themselves" (George Weigel, *Soul of the World: Notes on the Future of Public Catholicism* [Washington, DC, 1996], 109). On the subject of the subsidiarity principle see Peter L. Berger and Richard John Neuhaus, *To Empower People: The Role of Mediating Structures and Public Policy* (Washington, DC, 1997), 157–201.

43. *Centesimus Annus*, 40.

44. *Laborem Exercens*, I, 2.

45. J. Bryan Hehir, "Reordering the World," in George Weigel, ed., *A New Worldly Order: John Paul II and Human Freedom* (Washington, D.C., 1992), 88.

46. *Centesimus Annus*, 19. The pope's description of post–World War II efforts best fits Germany and its "economic miracle," when politicians and economists from certain classical liberal circles set up a social market economy.

47. Ibid., 46.

48. Weigel, *Soul of the World*, 120. With regard to this notable change in the position of the popes, a reflection by Sir Michael Howard, reported by Weigel, reflects very well the Anglo-Saxon mentality and is worth reporting: "In a conversation in the mid-1980s, Sir Michael Howard, then the Regius Professor of Modern History at Oxford, suggested that there had been two great revolutions in the twentieth century. The first had taken place when Lenin's Bolsheviks expropriated the Russian people's revolution in November 1917. The other was going on even as we spoke: the transformation of the Roman Catholic Church from a bastion of the *ancien régime* into perhaps the world's foremost institutional defender of human rights. It was a fascinating reading of the history of our century. I also sensed, in Sir Michael's telling of the story, just a *soupcon* of surprise: fancy that—the Vatican as defender of the rights of man!" (Weigel, *Soul of the World*, 99).

49. *Centesimus Annus*, 44.

50. Ibid., 46.

51. Bernhard Sutor, *Politische Ethik: Gesamtdarstellung auf der Basis der Christlichen Gesellschaftslehre* (Zurich, 1992).

52. Hallowell justly remarked, "Although the conception of rights implies correlative duties, liberalism tended to emphasize the inalienable nature of these rights rather than the duties which these rights imply. As a matter of fact, the liberal endeavour to ground these rights in the empirical nature of man, in an effort to divorce them from any dependence upon theological considerations, ignored the fact, which soon became apparent, that such rights are not empirically demonstrable. In reality, the rights of man derive not from the empirically observable nature of man but from the fact that man is a spiritual being created in the image and likeness of God. Men have rights because they have responsibilities which transcend the demands of the natural world" (John H. Hallowell, *The Moral Foundation of Democracy* [Chicago, 1965], 81). Also worth remembering is that, according to Maritain, the justification for the transcendence of the person is already possible on the natural and philosophical level, which is especially

important in a pluralistic culture (Jacques Maritain, *Man and the State*, 155).

53. Milton Friedman published a commentary on the encyclical, quite full of praise, in the special supplement of National Review (24 June 1991). On the mention of absolute truth, however, he responds with these questions: "Whose truth are we talking about? Who establishes it? Is this an echo of the Spanish Inquisition?"

54. *Centesimus Annus*, 46. Juan Miguel Garrigues points out that "the liberal State, which has escaped from the tutelage of religious dogmatism, is always in peril of succumbing to the positivist dogmatism of statism which is secretly at the base of modern ideological totalitarianisms" (Juan Miguel Garrigues, *L'Église, la société libre et le communisme*, 34). Many classical liberal thinkers are aware of this danger. Thus Hayek declares (Law, 4), "It would seem that wherever democratic institutions ceased to be restrained by the tradition of the Rule of Law, they led not only to 'totalitarian democracy' but in due time even to a 'plebiscitary dictatorship'" (Friedrich A. Hayek, *The Political Order of a Free People*, vol. 3, *Law, Legislation and Liberty* [London, 1979], 4).

55. *Centesimus Annus*, 44.

56. "Liberalism conceived of society being composed of atomlike, autonomous individuals with will and interests peculiar to themselves. But to this anarchic conception of society it counterposed the belief in the existence of a transcendental order of truth which is accessible to man's natural reason and capable of evoking a moral response" (Hallowell, *The Moral Foundation of Democracy*, 73). Adam Smith wrote, of the requirements of justice, truth, moral purity, and faithfulness, "But upon the tolerable observance of these duties, depends the very existence of human society, which would crumble into nothing if mankind were not generally impressed with a reverence for those important rules of conduct. This reverence is still further advanced by an opinion which is first impressed by nature, and afterwards confirmed by reasoning and philosophy, that those important rules of morality are the commands and laws of the Deity, who will finally reward the obedient,

and punish the transgressors of their duty" (Adam Smith, *The Theory of Moral Sentiments* [1759], part 3, chap. 5).

57. Garrigues makes the following comment: "Following the spiritual crisis of the end of the Middle Ages, which is consummated by the breaking up of the unity of the Church and the wars of religion, following the *rabies theologica* of seventeenth century England (Puritanism) and France (repeal of the Edict of Nantes, violent polemics on Jansenism and Quietism), it became apparent to reasonable men that the common good of civil peace demanded that the legitimate state be, not a-religious and separated from the Church, but founded on a social consensus which did not include the ultimate dogmatic options of the confessions of religious faiths. Only such a state could demand reciprocal tolerance on the part of the antagonistic Church communities" (Juan Miguel Garrigues, *L'Église, la société libre et le communisme*, 41–42).

58. See the previously cited works of Maritain, Pangle, and Hallowell, as well as Alasdair MacIntyre, *After Virtue* (Notre Dame, 1984).

59. Böckenförde, 24.

60. This consensus is necessary but, as Hayek notes, might concern only basic values: "True general agreement, or even true agreement among a majority, will in a Great Society rarely extend beyond some general principles, and can be maintained only on such particular measures as can be known to most of its members" (Hayek, *Law, Legislation, and Liberty*, 17). This mutually shared ethical minimum is, however, a necessary condition. "No system is safe without strong moral ties, and democracy is the least safe, since here responsibility does not extend to all, but to a larger oligarchy than usual" (Owen Chadwick, "Democracy and Religion," in *Europa und die "Civil Society*," Castelgandolfo-Gesprache, vol. 4 [Stuttgart, 1991], 142).

61. "A society of free men implies basic tenets which are at the core of its very existence. A genuine democracy implies a fundamental agreement between minds and wills on the bases of life in common; it is aware of itself and of its principles, and it must be capable of defending and promoting its own conception of social and political life" (Jacques Maritain, *Man and the State*, 109). More

and more often today, liberal political philosophers are recognizing this. It is worth citing Francis Fukuyama here: "If the institutions of democracy and capitalism are to work properly, they must coexist with certain premodern cultural habits that ensure their proper functioning. Law, contract, and economic rationality provide a necessary but not sufficient basis for both the stability and prosperity of postindustrial societies; they must as well be leavened with reciprocity, moral obligation, duty toward community, and trust, which are based in habit rather than rational calculation. The latter are not anachronisms in a modern society but rather the sine qua non of the latter's success" (Francis Fukuyama, *Trust: The Social Virtues and the Creation of Prosperity* [New York, 1995], 11).

62. Sutor, 197.

63. Note the remarks of Francis Fukuyama on the crisis of contemporary liberal democracies stemming from a disbelief in the possibility of rationally understanding man (Fukuyama, *Trust*, 139–43).

64. Hallowell, 107.

65. Michael Novak, *Free Persons and the Common Good* (Lanham, MD, 1988).

66. Hallowell, 115.

67. Hayek, *Law, Legislation, and Liberty*, 99. This is how Maritain explains the erosion of the nineteenth-century liberal state and the era of totalitarianism: "The mistake of bourgeois liberalism has been to conceive democratic society to be a kind of lists or arena in which all the conceptions of the bases of common life, even those most destructive to freedom and law, meet with no more than the pure and simple indifference of the body politic, while they compete before public opinion in a kind of free market of the mother-ideas, healthy or poisoned, of political life. Nineteenth century bourgeois democracy was *neutral* even with regard to freedom. Just as it had no real common good, it had no real *common thought*—no brains of its own, but a neutral, empty skull clad with mirrors: no wonder that before the second world war in countries that fascist, racist, or communist propaganda was to disturb or corrupt, it had become a society without any idea of itself, without any *common*

faith which could enable it to resist disintegration" (Maritain, *Man and the State*, 109–10).

68. Giovanni Sartori, *The Theory of Democracy Revisited*, part 1, The Contemporary Debate (New Jersey, 1987), 32.

69. Anthony Arblaster, *Democracy*, 3rd ed. (Buckingham, 2002), 71.

70. Hayek, *Law, Legislation and Liberty*, 17.

71. Maritain, *Man and the State*, 109.

72. Ibid., 110.

73. Ernst-Wolfgang Böckenförde, 120.

74. Francis Fukuyama, *The End of History and the Last Man* (New York, 1992), 326.

75. *Centesimus Annus*, 46.

76. According to Cardinal Ratzinger, "Democracy cannot function without values and thus cannot be neutral with regard to values. The formal element of its institutions is linked to the material element of an ethos that belongs to the Socratic and Christian tradition. Behind its formal obligations one comes across the more profound element of this moral obligation and constraint that the state must presuppose but cannot itself justify and thereby cannot itself guarantee" (Cardinal Joseph Ratzinger, Church, Ecumenism and Politics [New York, 1988], 188).

77. *Centesimus Annus*, 29.

CHAPTER 3: ECONOMIC LIFE

1. *Centesimus Annus*, 4.

2. Ibid., 5.

3. Ibid., 10, 5, 4.

4. "Manchester already seemed a vision of hell. Its population had increased tenfold between 1760 and 1830, rising from 17,000 to 180,000 inhabitants. Because of land shortage, the factories perched on its hills had five, six, or even twelve storeys. Mansions and workers' two-ups-two-downs sprawled all over the town, higgledy-piggledy. There were puddles and mud everywhere: for every paved street, there were ten dirty lanes. Men, women, and chil-

dren herded into squalid housing—up to 15 or 16 people might be crammed into a single basement; the 50,000 Irish immigrants were part of a typically wretched sub-proletariat" (Fernand Braudel, *Civilization and Capitalism, 15th–18th Century*, vol. 3, *The Perspective of the World* [Berkeley: University of California Press, 1992], 564–65).

5. Wilhelm Röpke, *The Social Crisis of Our Time* (New Brunswick, NJ: Transaction, 1992), 67.

6. Peter Berger, *The Capitalist Revolution: Fifty Propositions about Prosperity, Equality, and Liberty* (New York: Basic Books, 1986), 44. The response to the tragedy of the *Titanic* (1912), analyzed by Owen Chadwick, furnishes a remarkable illustration of Berger's thesis. The press of the day "felt it to have been a sin like the Tower of Babel; a monster effort at material luxury, £780 for the most expensive cabins, and just that week the miners' strike for a wage of 30 shillings a week desolated the country. One cabin for six days equal to ten men's wages for a year" (Owen Chadwick, *The Secularization of the European Mind in the Nineteenth Century* [New York: Cambridge University Press, 1977], 261).

7. "Between two-thirds and three-quarters of the workers in the early factories were under the age of eighteen, lucky if they earned halfpenny an hour, and for this being made to work as children had never been made to work before, eleven hours a day being the norm" (Rodger Charles, SJ, with Drostan MacLaren, OP, *The Social Teaching of Vatican II* [San Francisco: Ignatius Press, 1982], 270).

8. Charles and MacLaren, *The Social Teaching of Vatican II*, 270–71.

9. *Centesimus Annus*, 8, 4, 14, 13.

10. Richard H. Tawney, *Religion and the Rise of Capitalism* (New York, 1926), 10–11.

11. Here, though, Charles and MacLaren are right to add, "Children had been exploited before industrialization. What was new was that they were herded into factories and the cruelties inflicted on them were, according to the conventional wisdom, justifiable in the name of economic laws." Charles and MacLaren, *The Social Teaching of Vatican II*, 270.

12. Nathan Rosenberg and L. E. Birdzell Jr., *How the West Grew Rich:*

The Economic Transformation of the Industrial World (New York: Basic Books, 1986), 173. Fernand Braudel, who has titled one of the subchapters of his work "Industry, Providential Refuge from Poverty," notes that in the seventeenth and eighteenth centuries, the hiring of masses of part-time workers (seasonal workers, such as agricultural hands or fishermen) in a rising industry helped them survive (Braudel, *Civilization and Capitalism*, 307).

13. Christopher Dawson, *Progress and Religion: An Historical Inquiry* (Washington, DC: Catholic University Press, 2001), 162.

14. Wilhelm Röpke writes of a fourfold rise in the real wages of the English worker during the nineteenth century (Röpke, *The Social Crisis of Our Time*, 108).

15. Braudel raises a caveat about such a statement, emphasizing that it was not until 1850 that one could really speak of a permanent improvement in the condition of the proletariat (see Braudel, *Civilization and Capitalism*, 569). By contrast, Rosenberg and Birdzell conclude that, aside from the anomalies of Napoleonic times, "the factory system improved the average condition of workers from the beginning" (Rosenberg and Birdzell, *How the West Grew Rich*, 175). Even if, largely due to the narrow database, there is some disagreement among economic historians about the first half of the nineteenth century, then "controversy among historians diminishes greatly as one turns to the period since the middle of the nineteenth century. Here, there is little doubt: There occurred an immense increase in the material well-being of virtually all strata in Western societies, proceeding steadily despite some severe disruptions (notably the two world wars and the Great Depression), and then spurting forward dramatically after World War II" (Berger, *The Capitalist Revolution*, 41).

16. T. S. Ashton, "The Standard of Life of the Workers in England, 1790–1830," in F. A. Hayek, ed., *Capitalism and the Historians* (Chicago, 1954), 153–55.

17. *Centesimus Annus*, 5.

18. As the distinguished Austrian economist Joseph Schumpeter noted, "Queen Elizabeth owned silk stockings. The capitalist achievement does not typically consist in providing more silk

stockings for queens but in bringing them within reach of factory girls in return for steadily decreasing amounts of effort" (Joseph Schumpeter, *Capitalism, Socialism and Democracy* [New York, 1942].)

19. *Centesimus Annus*, 33.
20. Ibid., 39, 40, 42.
21. Ibid., 39, 29, 41.
22. Ibid., 36.
23. Ibid., 29.
24. Ibid., 39.
25. Ibid., 36.
26. Ibid., 41, 55.
27. Ibid., 19.
28. Milton Friedman, "The Social Responsibility of Business Is to Increase Its Profits," *New York Times Magazine*, September 13, 1970.
29. Ayn Rand, *Capitalism: The Unknown Ideal* (New York: Signet, 1986), 16.
30. "To the glory of mankind, there was, for the first and only time in history, a country of money—and I have no higher, more reverent tribute to pay to America, for this means: a country of reason, justice, freedom, production, achievement" (Ayn Rand, *For the New Intellectual* [New York: Signet, 1963], 93).
31. "A proper government is only a policeman, acting as an agent of man's self-defense. . . . The only proper functions of a government are: the police, to protect you from criminals; the army, to protect you from foreign invaders; and the courts" (Ayn Rand, *Atlas Shrugged* [New York: Plume, 1999 (1957)], 1062).
32. Robert Nozick, *Anarchy, State, and Utopia* (New York, 1974), 181.
33. This has been well analyzed by Daniel Bell. See, for instance, *The Cultural Contradictions of Capitalism*, part 1, chap. 1.
34. Jean Baudrillard, *Selected Writings*, ed. Mark Poster (Stanford: Stanford University Press, 2011), 32.
35. Susan Meld Shell, "Preserving the Humanities: Address to the Madison Center Conference on the Humanities," Washington DC, 10 Oct. 1989, as cited in Thomas L. Pangle, *The Ennobling of*

Democracy: The Challenge of the Postmodern Age (Baltimore: Johns Hopkins, 1992), 19.

36. *Centesimus Annus*, 36.
37. Ibid.
38. Ibid., 39.
39. Ibid., 32, 42.
40. Ibid., 31, 32.
41. Ibid., 32.
42. Ibid., 32.
43. The Polish professor (later bishop) Marian Jaworski first suggested this terminology to me. See Maciej Zięba, *The Surprising Pope: Understanding the Thought of John Paul II* (Lanham, MD: Lexington Books, 2000), 22.
44. *Centesimus Annus*, 43, 40, 41, 32, 43, 35.
45. These explicit affirmations allow us to stress the total difference between profit, on the one hand, and exploitation and usury. This distinction, which has had significant repercussions on the attitude of Catholics to the economy, has been often misunderstood within the Church from ancient times until the present day. See Jacques Le Goff, *La bourse et la vie: économie et la religion au Moyen Âge* (Paris, 1997).
46. *Centesimus Annus*, 30.
47. Ibid., 30, 43.
48. Ibid., 19.
49. Ibid.
50. Ibid., 35, 25.
51. Röpke, *A Humane Economy*, 25.
52. Röpke, *The Social Crisis of Our Time*, 53.
53. Ibid., 119.
54. Ibid., 120. That is why the Ordoliberals were accustomed to saying that the economy was not wild vegetation (*Naturgewächs*) but rather a cultivated crop (*Kulturpflanze*).
55. Röpke, *The Moral Foundations of Civil Society*, 32.
56. As Müller-Armack wrote, "This is an idea of the political order that has for its goal to enter into partnership, exactly on the basis of an economy of competition and free initiative, with a guaranteed

social progress by the acquisitions of the market economy. Founded on the order of the market economy, a multiform and complete system of social protection is possible" (A. Müller-Armack, "Soziale Marktwirtschaft—Ordnung der Zukunft," in Erwin von Beckerath, ed., *Handwörterbuch der Sozialwissenschaften: zugleich Neuauflage des Handwörterbuch der Staatswissensschaften* [Frankfurt-Main-Berlin-Wien, 1972]).

57. See especially Röpke, *The Social Crisis of Our Time*. For a helpful overview of Röpke's thought in this area, see Gerrit Meijer, "Some Aspects of the Relationship between the Freiburg School and the Austrian School," in Jürgen G. Backhaus, ed., *Modern Applications of Austrian Thought* (New York: Routledge, 2005), 143–45.

58. "Uncontrolled competition has a tendency to self-liquidation": Müller-Armack, "Soziale Marktwirtschaft," 269. "It is typical of that period of enlightenment that what was in reality a highly fragile artificial product of civilization was held to be a natural growth. One was, therefore, basically inclined to acknowledge no bounds to economic freedom, and to range again into the Unconditional and Absolute, granting only grudgingly, and in moments of weakness, the concessions which stark reality finally demanded. One refused to see that a market economy needs a firm moral, political and institutional framework (a minimum standard of business ethics, a strong state, a sensible 'market police,' and well weighed laws appropriate to the economic system), if it was not to fail and at the same time destroy society as a whole by permitting the unbridled rule of vested interests. Historical liberalism (particularly the nineteenth century brand), never understood that competition is a dispensation, by no means harmless from a moral and sociological point of view; it has to be kept within bounds and watched if it is not to poison the body politic" (Röpke, *The Social Crisis of Our Time*, 52).

59. Gustav Stolper, *German Realities* (New York: Reynal and Hitchcock, 1948), 22.

60. The French economists Jacques Rueff and André Piettre, who are undoubtedly biased, nonetheless vividly described the effects of this reform: "The black market suddenly disappeared. Shop

windows were full of goods; factory chimneys were smoking and the streets swarmed with lorries. Everywhere the noise of new buildings going up replaced the deathly silence of the ruins. If the state of recovery was a surprise, its swiftness was even more so. In all sectors of economic life it began as the clocks struck on the day of currency reform" (Quoted in Ludwig Erhard, *Prosperity Through Competition* [New York: Frederick A. Praeger, 1958], 13).

61. See *Centesimus Annus*, 8. As Röpke observed, "On a par with this rationalist exaggeration of the competitive principle, based on the egoism of each individual, was the sociological blindness through which the individual was thought to be an isolated, atomized entity who could as such be made the basis of the economy; all the indispensable cohesive forces of the family and the natural social groups (the neighborhood, the parish, occupation, &c.), were considered irksome fetters. In this way that questionable form of individualism was evolved which in the end has proved to be a menace to society and has so discredited a fundamentally sound idea as to further the rise of the far more dangerous collectivism" (Röpke, *The Social Crisis of Our Time*, 52).

62. *Centesimus Annus*, 13, 14, 23, 24, 12.

63. Ibid., 39.

64. Röpke, *The Moral Foundations of Civil Society*, 133.

65. Campanini would write: "When it comes to a holistic appraisal of capitalism, it is only since John Paul II's *Centesimus annus* that a change in perspective has taken place." Further on, he adds, "Catholic social thinking has shifted from rejection or even demonization of capitalism to attitudes more reflexive and sensitive" (G. Campanini, "La cultura del mondo cattolico di fronte al capitalismo," *La Societa*, 1995, n. 2, 320, 326).

66. John O'Sullivan, "The Pope, Liberty, and Capitalism: Essays on *Centesimus Annus*," *National Review*, June 24, 1991.

67. This group of intellectuals, arising in the United States in the 1970s, differed from the Ordoliberals in that they did not aspire to create an economic program and there were no prominent politicians among them. Like the Ordoliberals, however, they connected the experiences of economists, philosophers, historians of ideas,

writers, and theologians to formulate a diagnosis of the current time; the neoconservative synthesis was similar in its framework to the diagnosis of the postwar German reformers. Some of the best-known representatives of neoconservatism have been Peter Berger, Irving Kristol, George Gilder, Gertrude Himmelfarb, Joshua Muravchik, Richard J. Neuhaus, Michael Novak, Norman Podhoretz, and George Weigel.

68. "Virtually all political questions today revolve around economic ones. . . . But economics is not what it appears to be in either; it is grounded in social life and cannot be understood separately from the larger question of how modern societies organize themselves" (Francis Fukuyama, *Trust: The Social Virtues and the Creation of Prosperity* [New York: Free Press, 1995], xiii).

CHAPTER 4: THE PRIMACY OF CULTURE

1. *Centesimus Annus*, 51.
2. Ibid., 46, 36.
3. A deep examination of this subject, one that encompasses a theological perspective, can be found in the section "Towards the Definition of Culture" in H. Richard Niebuhr, *Christ and Culture* (New York, 1951), 29–39.
4. *Gaudium et Spes*, 53.
5. Ibid.
6. *Centesimus Annus*, 39.
7. Ibid., 13, 24, 38.
8. Ibid., 13.
9. Allan Bloom, *The Closing of the American Mind: How Higher Education Has Failed Democracy and Impoverished the Souls of Today's Students* (New York, 1987), 185.
10. Niebuhr, *Christ and Culture*, 69.
11. *Centesimus Annus*, 36, 24, 41.
12. T. S. Eliot, *Christianity and Culture: The Idea of a Christian Society and Notes towards the Definition of Culture* (New York, 1968), 170.
13. *Centesimus Annus*, 38, 41, 58, 36.

14. An original description and a classical example is J. B. Bury, *The Idea of Progress* (New York, 1955). On the other hand, Robert Nisbet's *History of the Idea of Progress* (New York: Basic Books, 1980) constitutes a remarkable critical exposition of this idea.

15. Daniel Bell, *The Cultural Contradictions of Capitalism* (New York: Basic Books, 1976), 34.

16. Ibid.

17. Ibid., 107–8, 72.

18. Bell writes, "Culture, for a society, a group, or a person, is a continual process of sustaining an identity" (Bell, *The Cultural Contradictions of Capitalism*, 70). Niebuhr observes: "The systems of laws and liberties, the customs of social intercourse, the methods of thought, the institutions of learning and religion, the techniques of art, of language, and of morality itself—these cannot be conserved by keeping in repair the walls and documents that are their symbols. They need to be written afresh generation by generation 'on the tables of the heart.' Let education and training lapse for one generation, and the whole grand structure of past achievements falls into ruin. Culture is social tradition which must be conserved by painful struggle not so much against nonhuman natural forces as against revolutionary and critical powers in human life and reason" (Niebuhr, *Christ and Culture*, 37). The pope writes of culture in analogous terms, though he is more optimistic about the significance of cultural confrontation.

19. *Centesimus Annus*, 24, 13.

20. *Gaudium et Spes*, 24. Of course, this is a classical thesis of Catholic theology. See, e.g., St. Thomas Aquinas, *Summa Contra Gentiles* 3:112: "The intellectual nature is the only one that is required in the universe, for its own sake, while all others are for its sake."

21. *Centesimus Annus*, 53 (see *Redemptor Hominis*, 13), 13.

22. Ibid., 24, 13.

23. As T. S. Eliot observed, "The fact that culture has become, in some sense, a department of politics, should not obscure in our memory the fact that at other periods politics has been an activity pursued within a culture, and between representatives of different cultures." See Eliot, *Christianity and Culture*, 158.

24. *Centesimus Annus*, 49.

25. C. Caffara, "Dottrina Sociale della Chiesa. Giustificazione teologica," *Communio*, ed. italienne, n. 56, March–April 1981, 7.

26. *Centesimus Annus*, 49, 50.

27. Ibid., 50.

28. Ibid., 41.

29. Hans Urs von Balthasar, *Theo-Drama: Theological Dramatic Theory*, vol. 5, *The Dramatis Personae: The Person in Christ* (San Francisco: Ignatius Press, 1992), 207.

30. *Centesimus Annus*, 41, 29.

31. See, for example, *Centesimus Annus*, 3, 5, 6, 9, 11, 13, 14, 22, 29, 33, 43, 44, 49, 60, 61.

32. Ibid., 22, 44, 54.

33. One must agree with Paul Ricoeur, who notes, "The gap can no longer be bridged, the gap which exists between a subject who posits himself as the origin of values and a world which unfolds itself as a collection of appearances stripped of all value. . . . Nihilism is the historical verification of this impossibility" (Paul Ricoeur, The *Conflict of Interpretations* [Evanston, 1974], 463).

34. *Centesimus Annus*, 11, 53, 13, 55, 24, 39–40, 37.

35. Ibid., 49, 27.

36. Jerzy Szacki, *Spotkania z utopia*, Warsaw, 1980, 210–11.

37. *Centesimus Annus*, 46, 29.

38. Ibid., 4, 17.

39. "Humanitarianism is the peculiar possession of a people who have worshipped for centuries the Divine Humanity—apart from all that even our humanism would have been other than it is" (Dawson, *Progress and Religion*, 187).

40. *Centesimus Annus*, 29.

41. Nikolaus Lobkowicz, *Czas kryzysu, czas przełomu* (Kraków, 1996), 105.

42. Leszek Kołakowski, *Religion* (New York: Oxford University Press, 1982), 214–15.

43. Jan Patočka, "Czy dzieje maja sens?" *Znak*, 257/258 (November–December 1975): 1396–1414. Let us recall Kołakowski's conclusion: "Without the all-encompassing truth there is no fragmentary one; and the all-encompassing truth presupposes an infinite omniscient

intelligence" (Kołakowski, *Religion*, 83). "It seems that the question of meaning ... is void and illegitimate unless a channel is open to us whereby we can make contact with the eternal repository of meanings" (Kołakowski, *Religion*, 155).

44. Kołakowski, *Religion*, 214–15.
45. *Centesimus Annus*, 13, 31, 32, 43, 6.
46. Ibid., 43, 41.
47. Mariano Fazio, "Autonomia assoluta versus autonomia relativa," in *La Società*, no. 2 (1995): 313.
48. *Centesimus Annus*, 41, 43, 22, 61.
49. *Rerum Novarum*, 42, cited in *Centesimus Annus*, 10.
50. Ibid., 10, 11, 57.
51. Ibid., 13, 41.
52. Ibid., 11, 59, 55.
53. Ibid., 38–39.
54. Ibid., 53, 51, 38.
55. Ibid., 54.
56. Ibid., 25.
57. Such a statement does not require a theological justification. This view has been shared by distinguished theorists of the "open society" such as Karl Popper. Bertrand Russell—openly antagonistic toward Christianity—spent most of his life constructing a coherent and durable system of rational ethics. Toward the end of his life, however, he declared that such a system is impossible to construct without an "ethical axiom" (and therefore without reference to a transcendent truth): "An ethical opinion can only be defended by an ethical axiom, but, if the axiom is not accepted, there is no way of reaching a rational conclusion." See Bertrand Russell, *The Autobiography of Bertrand Russell*, vol. 3 (London, 1969), 33.
58. *Centesimus Annus*, 44, 46, 17.
59. Ibid., 32.
60. Ibid., 38.
61. In a wonderful monograph on the contribution of Christian anthropology to the self-consciousness of our civilization, William M. Thompson suggests that, thanks to Christ, "I" has become radically aware of its spiritual and transcendental nature. See William M.

Thompson, *Christ and Consciousness: Exploring Christ's Contribution to Human Consciousness* (New York: Paulist Press, 1977), 66–67. For this reason the pope feels that the Church's essential contribution to the democratic order is "precisely her vision of the dignity of the person revealed in all its fullness in the mystery of the Incarnate Word" (*Centesimus Annus*, 47).

62. Romano Guardini, *Angefochtene Zuversicht. Romano Guardini Lesenbuch* (Mainz: Matthias-Grunewald Verlag, 1985), part 2. Guardini devotes many of his deliberations to demonstrating the lack of integrity of our time in wishing to separate the person from his foundations. "Modern man's dishonesty was rooted in his refusal to recognize Christianity's affirmation of the God-man relationship. Even as the modern world acclaimed the worth of personality and of an order of personal values, it did away with their guarantor, Christian Revelation. . . . An uprooted personal culture is powerless against the breakthrough of positivism" (Romano Guardini, *The End of the Modern World* [Wilmington, DE: ISI Books, 1998], 99–100).

This process has lasted over subsequent decades, Guardini emphasizes, and, as a distinguished representative of the subsequent intellectual generation, noted that since the nineteenth century, the ideal "individual needing nothing but his own inner resources to the desocialized, hedonistic, narcissistic free spirit of the late twentieth century is really not a long journey" (Robert Nisbet, *Prejudices: A Philosophical Dictionary* [Cambridge, MA, 1982], 187).

63. *Centesimus Annus*, 22.
64. A. Szostek, *Wokól godnosci, prawdy i milosci* (Redakcja Wydawnictw KUL: Lublin, 1995), 39.
65. See Jaroslaw Kupczak, *The Human Person as an Efficient Cause in the Christian Anthropology of Karol Wojtyla* (Washington, DC, 1960), 140ff.
66. *Centesimus Annus*, 6, 15.
67. Ibid., 25.
68. Ibid., 46, 49, 50, 46.
69. Ibid., 50.

70. Ibid., 32, 42, 36.
71. Röpke, *The Social Crisis of Our Time*, 52.
72. Friedrich A. von Hayek, "The Moral Element in Free Enterprise," in *The Morality of Capitalism*, ed. M. W. Hendrickson (New York, 1992), 73.
73. *Centesimus Annus*, 34, 40.
74. Ibid., 46, 13, 35, 25.
75. Ibid., 25.
76. "It must not be forgotten that, if Abraham's faith can be defined as 'for God everything is possible,' the faith of Christianity implies that everything is also possible for man" (Mircea Eliade, *The Myth of the Eternal Return: or, Cosmos and History* [New Haven, 1971], 160).
77. *Centesimus Annus*, 26, 43, 29.

CONCLUSION: FROM CENTESIMUS ANNUS TO CARITAS IN VERITATE

1. *Caritas in Veritate*, 8.
2. *Sollicitudo Rei Socialis*, 41.
3. Ibid., 5.
4. Ibid., 26.
5. Ibid., 24, 25, see 32.
6. Ibid., 21, see 40.
7. Ibid., 33, 40.
8. Ibid., 40.
9. Ibid., 25, 64.
10. Ibid., 9.
11. Ibid., 21, 32, 40, 53, 19, 41.
12. For example, the pope calls for reform of the United Nations and of economic and finance institutions "so that the concept of the family of nations can acquire real teeth" (*Caritas in Veritate*, 67). As appealing as this concept is, what sort of reform could achieve it in the modern world, which is deeply divided and predominantly undemocratic? How to establish peaceful coexistence among

nations and protect human rights in all countries in a world where there is Cuba and Sudan, North Korea and Iran, Afghanistan and Belarus, Russia and China, Georgia, and Syria, and where some Arab countries call the United States "the Great Satan"?

13. *Caritas in Veritate*, 35, 34, 36, 24, 39, 42, 57.

14. Ibid., 49.

15. Ibid., 67.

16. Ibid., 47, 60, 24, 38, 39, 57, 47, 43.

17. "CWR Round-Table: *Caritas in Veritate*," *Catholic World Report*, July 9, 2009.

18. George Weigel, "*Caritas in Veritate* in Gold and Red: The Revenge of Justice and Peace (or So They May Think)," *National Review Online*, July 7, 2009, www.nationalreview.com/node/227839.

19. Ibid.

20. *Caritas in Veritate*, 14, 22.

21. Ibid., 41, 32.

22. "CWR Round-Table: *Caritas in Veritate.*"

23. Weigel, "*Caritas in Veritate* in Gold and Red."

24. On this sort of "natural" illusory sympathy of Christianity for socialism, Irving Kristol observes: "The trouble . . . is that socialism offers a redistribution that only looks like Christian charity, and that socialist societies, when they come into being, are but grotesque parodies of a Christian community. One major reason why this is so is that the socialist promise is not truly a Christian promise. It promises redistribution *and* prosperity—and on this promise it simply cannot deliver" (Irving Kristol, *Reflections of a Neoconservative* [New York: Basic Books, 1983], 437).

25. As Johannes Schasching aptly observes: "One could regret that cultural institutions, and especially the Church, have not been able to correct this erroneous behavior [consumerism], but this should not become an accusation against this economic system" (J. Schasching, *Unterwegs mit den Menschen. Kommentar zur Enzyklika Centesimus annus von Johannes Paulus II* [Vienna: Europa Verlag, 1991], 90).

26. Walter Kasper, *The Christian Understanding of Freedom and the History of Freedom in the Modern Era: The Meeting and Confrontation*

between Christianity and the Modern Era in a Postmodern Situation
(Milwaukee: Marquette University Press, 1988), 43–44.

27. Ibid., 40.

28. Guardini describes the verital society of pre-Enlightenment
Europe: "During the Middle Ages life was interwoven with religion
at every level and in every ramification. For all men the Christian
Faith represented the generally accepted truth. In some manner
everything was stamped by Christianity and the Church: the social
order, legislation, the ethos governing public and private life, the
speculations of philosophy, artistic endeavors and the historic climate within which all idea moved. Even while including all these
things, we do not begin to indicate the cultural values won for the
personality of man through this mingling of the cultural and the
religious. Even injustice itself stood measured and condemned by
Christianity" (Romano Guardini, *The End of the Modern World*
[Wilmington, DE: ISI Books, 1998], 95).

29. John H. Hallowell, *The Moral Foundation of Democracy* (Chicago:
University of Chicago Press, 1965), 70.

30. John Locke, *Concerning Civil Government, Second Essay*, II, 12.

31. Hallowell, *The Moral Foundation of Democracy*, 72.

32. As Claude Gilbert penned in 1700, as a sort of Enlightenment creed,
"By obeying reason we depend on no one but ourselves and so, in
a sense, we, too, become gods" (as cited in Paul Hazard, *The Crisis
of the European Mind, 1680–1715* [New York: New York Review of
Books, 2013], 141).

33. Guardini, *The End of the Modern World*, 97.

34. Paul Hazard, *European Thought in the Eighteenth Century: From
Montesquieu to Lessing* (New Haven, CT: Yale University Press),
64–65. Anticlericalism became an integral element in the building
of the new Enlightenment order. Hazard writes: "That the eighteenth century witnessed the birth of a race of men, thereafter per-
petuated, whose sole spiritual nourishment was anti-clericalism,
who made anti-clericalism the sole item on their programme,
and who deemed that that would suffice to remodel governments, to perfect societies, and lead the way to happiness—for
this, many men are responsible—and not all of them belong to the

Encyclopaedist camp." But "none of them," Hazard concludes, was responsible "to the same degree as Voltaire." See Hazard, *European Thought in the Eighteenth Century*, 415.

35. Dawson, *Progress and Religion*, 168.

36. J. F. Lyotard, *La condition postmoderne* (Paris: Les Editions de Minuit, 1979); Richard Rorty, *Contingency, Irony, and Solidarity* (Cambridge: Cambridge University Press, 1989).

37. See, besides Hallowell and Guardini, Arnold Toynbee's essay "Christianity and Civilization," in which the author writes: "Democracy is another leaf from the book of Christianity, which has also, I fear, been torn out. . . . Practice unsupported by belief is a wasting asset, as we have suddenly discovered, to our dismay, in this generation" (Arnold Toynbee, *Civilisation on Trial* [London: Oxford University Press, 1957], 236).

38. Richard Rorty writes, "If we take care of political freedom, truth and goodness will take care of themselves." See Rorty, *Contingency, Irony, and Solidarity*, 84). See also Ernest Gellner, *Postmodernism, Reason, and Religion* (New York: Routledge, 2001): "Postmodernism would seem to be rather clearly in favour of relativism, in as far as it is capable of clarity, and hostile to the idea of unique, exclusive, objective, external or transcendent truth. Truth is elusive, polymorphous, inward, subjective . . . and perhaps a few further things as well."

39. Robert Nisbet wrote: "But is this contemporary Western culture likely to continue for long? The answer, it seems to me, must be in the negative—if we take any stock in the lessons of the human past. One cannot be certain, of course; there is no sure way of catapulting ourselves into the future; no way of being confident that even the hardiest or most promising of current trends will continue indefinitely. But we can take some reasonable guidance, I believe, first from the fact that never in history have periods of culture such as our own lasted for very long. They are destroyed by all the forces which constitute their essence. How can any society or age last very long if it lacks or is steadily losing the minimal requirements for a society—such requirements being the very opposite of the egocentric and hedonistic elements which dominate Western

culture today? Second, it is impossible to overlook at the present time a phenomenon that as recently as the 1940s we thought so improbable as to be unworthy of serious thought or discussion. I refer to the faint, possibly illusory, signs of the beginning of a religious renewal in Western civilization, notably in America. Whatever their future, the signs are present—visible in the currents of fundamentalism, pentecostalism, even millennialism found in certain sectors of Judaism and Christianity." See Nisbet, *The History of the Idea of Progress*, 356.

40. See Benjamin R. Barber, *Jihad vs. McWorld* (New York: Ballantine Books, 1996); Samuel P. Huntington, *The Clash of Civilizations and the Remaking of World Order* (New York: Touchstone, 1996); Zbigniew Brzezinski, *Out of Control: Global Turmoil on the Eve of the Twenty-First Century* (New York: Scribner, 1993).

41. Samuel P. Huntington, "The Clash of Civilizations?" *Foreign Affairs* (Summer 1993).

42. Toynbee, *Civilisation on Trial*, 236–37.

43. *Centesimus Annus*, 46.

AFTERWORD FOR THE PAPERBACK EDITION:
POPE FRANCIS AND THE CRISIS OF THE MODERN ECONOMY

1. "Rush Limbaugh vs. Pope Francis: Talk Show Host Attacks 'Pure Marxism' of 'Evangelii Gaudium,'" *Huffington Post*, December 2, 2013, www.huffingtonpost.com/2013/12/02/rush-limbaugh-pope-francis_n_4373635.html; Henry Cox, "Is Pope Francis the New Champion of Liberation Theology?" *The Nation*, January 6–13, 2014.

2. Robert Calderisi, "Radical Pope, Traditional Values," *New York Times*, December 29, 2013.

3. *Evangelii Gaudium*, 55; *Centesimus Annus*, 39.

4. Calderisi, "Radical Pope, Traditional Values."

INDEX

INTERCOLLEGIATE
STUDIES INSTITUTE
Educating for Liberty

ISI Books is the publishing imprint of the Intercollegiate Studies Institute (ISI). Since its founding in 1953, ISI has been inspiring college students to discover, embrace, and advance the principles and virtues that make America free and prosperous.

Today ISI has more than 10,000 student members on college campuses across the country. The Institute reaches these and thousands of other people through an integrated program of campus speakers, conferences, seminars, publications, student groups, and fellowships and scholarships, along with a rich repository of online resources.

ISI is a nonprofit, nonpartisan, tax-exempt educational organization. The Institute relies on the financial support of the general public—individuals, foundations, and corporations—and receives no funding or any other aid from any level of the government.

To learn more about ISI,
visit www.isi.org or call (800) 526-7022